SPIRITUAL GROWTH

Don Clowers

WORD OF FAITH®
LEADERSHIP AND BIBLE INSTITUTE

PO Box 819000 • Dallas, Texas 75381

ISBN 0-914307-28-2

SPIRITUAL GROWTH

TABLE OF CONTENTS

FOREWARD

At the date of this writing, I have been in the service of the Lord for 25 years. Looking back over these years of my life in the ministry, I can recall many, many things which God has done for me and how I have grown in HIM as a result. I also remember mistakes that I have made and how that the majority of them could have been avoided if I had received proper training and instruction at an early stage.

I have experienced many disappointments, problems, and pains in the course of my life, but I continue to mature and develop as a Christian through taking God's Word and applying it to my daily life. This brings me to the purposes for which this book was written. They are to give you a guide in the steps to Christian maturity, to help you find somewhere within these covers answers to questions you may have had concerning steps you are already familiar with, to motivate you to DO what you have learned, to help you see that you can ultimately be the overcomer in all things which God intends for you to be. You can deal effectively with anything that comes your way!

INTRODUCTION

When I think of a new-born Christian, an infant comes to mind. There is a definite parallel between the two. When a child is born into this world he has all the physical organs and body parts that he will ever have. These parts are immature, though, a process of growth begins to take place. Even with the most basic nourishment the physical body will grow to adult stature. The mind, though, is different. If there is no stimulation, there is no growth. The capacity is there, but the lack of knowledge will truly destroy the fulfillment of that person's potential.

The same is true of a person who becomes born again. In my mind the same picture of an infant is there. When he accepts Jesus as his Savior, the new life of God comes into his spirit.

> *"Therefore if any man be in Christ, he is a new creature: old things are passed away, behold, all things are become new."* [II Corinthians 5:17]

ALL OF GOD'S LOVE SOURCE IS THERE---ALL OF GOD'S POWER SOURCE IS THERE. This supernatural potential is now there, but a new-born child of God has got to tap into it.

Some people expect new-born Christians to be able to do everything on their own. This is such a mistake. When a person is born again, whether it is in church, at a Bible Study, on a bus, on the phone, or in the street, the believer should obtain his name and address. He should then be directed where he can be discipled and receive teaching of the uncompromised gospel of Christ. He MUST BE helped and encouraged by other believers to walk in the new life! The mother of a newborn child does not put her baby to bed, give it its bottle, and say: "Feed yourself." She does not put diapers in the crib and say: "Change yourself." Of course she wouldn't. She loves her child and understands that even though it has hands, it does not yet know how to use them. She gladly holds the bottle for her baby, and does not complain but continually talks to her child.

She says cute things; things that to anyone else would be senseless yet she is communicating love by the tone of her voice and facial expression. She speaks to the child as if it is a baby, and not an adult. The mother does not expect the baby in its infant stage to say "Momma!"--rather she treats her baby like a baby. She holds it properly to keep it from falling, and makes sure that its head does not move back too far. It already has everything it needs in its body, but development must take place. The new birth is the same way. The source of God is in the recreated spirit. The spirit is reborn instantly, but the mind must be renewed to God's way of doing things.

New Christians should be nurtured, like babies. They should not be expected to do the things that mature Christians are expected to do. They must be given time to grow up and mature; the same way that you would give a baby time to grow up and find out what life is all about. This does not mean that it takes as much time for the new born child of God to grow up as it does the natural child to develop. A lot of the growth will depend on how much love, care, and proper teaching that the person gets from believers.

What I am saying is that you shouldn't say to them, "Well, if you're really saved, you'll come to church and grow up." Instead, make the effort to love them and share with them. Give them your time and tell them about your church. As a mother and father looks after their child, you should do the same with a new-born child of God. Little by little, teach them to do things on their own. They must be taught to pray, meditate, read the Word of God, go to church regularly, give of their time, and give of their substance.

My wife, Sharon, and I believe that we were very loving and patient parents. We were loving yet very firm with our four children. Tammy was our first child. We noticed EVERYTHING she did! We encouraged her to sit up, crawl, and take her first steps. As she tried to walk, we helped steady her, until she gained confidence in her own ability to take steps on her own. After Tammy was 10 months old, Sharon bought her a training cup. She told me that when Tammy became 11 months old, she was going to take her bottle away. She began teaching Tammy to drink from her training cup. The day Tammy was 11 months old, Sharon took the bottle from her. It was not that difficult for her, because she had already been learning to use the training cup and had developed the technique of drinking from it.

The new born child of God should be helped in this same way. People that are born again have made the decision to accept Jesus Christ. They make that decision on their own. We in turn must train them and then encourage them to take other steps on their own to grow up spiritually.

Chapter 1

THE NATURAL MAN

"But the natural man receiveth not the things of the Spirit of God: for they are foolishness unto him: neither can he know them, because they are spiritually discerned."
[I Corinthians 2:14]

The man who has never been born again is the natural man. He cannot understand the things of God, because he does not have God's life in him. **He is motivated by worldly things.** In other words, he is ruled by Satan. I'm not suggesting that he is demon possessed, only that the light of God has not come into his spirit. Thus his deeds are controlled by the god of this world who is Satan.

"But if our gospel be hid, it is hid to them that are lost: 4, In whom the god of this world hath blinded the minds of them which believe not, lest the light of the glorious gospel of Christ, who is the image of God, should shine unto them." [II Corinthians 4:3 & 4]

1

Paul is saying here that the man who has not accepted Jesus is blinded to the things of God; he is in darkness; he is lost. He learns everything by his five senses: hearing, seeing, tasting, smelling, and feeling. The person who is born again, though, has another method by which he learns and receives revelation knowledge; that is by the Spirit of God.

> *"The spirit of man is the candle of the Lord, searching all the inward parts of the belly."*
> *[Proverbs 20:27]*

When a person is born again, God's Spirit becomes united with his spirit. When he begins to read and meditate the Word of God, he understands how the Word of God is spiritually discerned or understood.

People told me that they have gone to church for years; some have been on deacon boards; others have been Music Directors; still others have been in almost every areas of the church yet they did not know Jesus as their personal Savior. This service was only a form or an act; it was not real. It could not be real until they asked Jesus into their life. Randy Gearhart, who is a good friend of mine and the Pastor of a church in Dublin, Georgia, is a classic example.

He told me that he attended church for two years, and during that time, he attained to the office of an elder and taught Sunday School. All this, yet he had no personal relationship with Jesus Christ. He said, "I was not even born again; I had never asked Jesus into my life!" He remarked that he did not know anything about the Bible, yet he taught a Sunday School Class! I asked him what he taught. He told me that he taught only a form of God, because he did not know God.

"Satan has made (men) blind, unable to see the glorious light of the gospel that is shining upon him,..." [II Corinthinas 4:4, The Living Bible]

Randy's eyes were blinded to spiritual things. You cannot begin to understand the spiritual things of God either, until His life is part of yours. In church he liked the dismissal prayer most of all. Why? Because what he was doing was a form, and he was bored.

Randy's wife was brought up in a different spiritual environment, and she continually witnessed to him. Other people outside of his church also witnessed to him, and his eyes were finally opened to the fact that he was practicing a form of religion. As a result, he became dissatisfied with the direction of his life, and one day he accepted Jesus Christ as Lord and Savior of his life--(after he had been called an elder and a Sunday School Teacher!) After his transformation and his receiving of the Holy Spirit, he had to go to another place of worship to have real fellowship. He could not stay where he had been, because they did not teach the things of God by experience. They only taught about God, **and there is a big difference!** He now pastors a successful Full Gospel Church and teaches people how to be born again by the Spirit of God.

It is a shame that many people feel as if everything is all right because they go to church. The real truth is that the natural man is without God; his wisdom is earthly or natural.

3

> *"But if ye have bitter envying and strife in your hearts, glory not, and lie not against the truth. 15, This wisdom descendeth not from above, but is earthly, sensual, devilish."*
> *[James 3:14 & 15]*

The natural man's wisdom is not from God. James says that he is motivated by selfishness, jealousy, envy, and strife. His daily life is filled with frustration, fear, and bitterness.

Think about this for a moment. Churches are run by people who have never let Jesus come into their lives. How can those who have never accepted Jesus into their own life help and encourage others in the things of God? They are only social gathering places because the gospel is hidden from them when their leaders are not born again. They are blinded from real revelation of God. I don't make this statement to be critical of others, but rather to open your eyes to pray for them.

The natural man obeys the passion of his senses, carries out the dictates of his flesh, and follows the prince of the power of the air. He is obedient to Satan and under his control, walking in the course of this world. This type of people have no inward life from God, as they are led by their feelings.

> *"And you hath He quickened, who were dead in trespasses and sins;*
> *2, Wherein in time past ye walked according to the course of this world, according to the prince of the power of the air, the spirit that now worketh in the children of disobedience:*
> *3, Among whom also we all had our conversation in times past in the lusts of our flesh,*

4

fulfilling the desires of the flesh and of the mind; and were by nature the children of wrath, even as others." [Ephesians 2:1-3]

Paul is saying here that the unborn man is actually following the devil, because he is by nature a child of wrath and disobedience. Darkness is inside him, and his conversation and thoughts are in the world. He seeks and follows worldly things because he is not interested in the things of God.

Let me say here that some people are turned off to God, because they are told all of the things that they cannot do when they become a Christian. This is the wrong approach to win a person to Jesus Christ. I grew up in a strict Pentecostal Church. I was afraid of God; I was always running away from God instead of running to Him! I went to church and was told all of the things that I could not do. The result was that I did not get a picture of a loving and kind God. Women were told they could not cut their hair, wear make up, or slacks. I was told that I could not go swimming in public, or go to the movies. My impression of accepting Jesus into my life meant giving up good times. When I did pray, it was out of fear of going to hell; not because of my love for God. However, the time came when I made a quality decision to serve the Lord because I wanted to! This time there was a joy in serving Him! I did not want to go to hell, and neither should anyone; but that should not be the only reason for someone to come to Christ. You must come to Him because you really want His love, His life, and His wisdom. When you come to Him because it is the desire of your heart, it's a real commitment!

Wherever you are, or whatever you may have done, **God accepts you where you are!** It is not discontinuing doing things, but the acceptance of what Jesus has done for you. He comes into your life when you accept Him as your Lord, and he doesn't hold anything against you! Don't try to change people, let God do that. When a person accepts Jesus, the old things pass away, and all things become new. The change in your spirit comes immediately--but the change in your mind comes perpetually. It's really like fishing—first, you **catch** the fish, then you **clean** it! Some people try to clean people, **then** get them saved. But the first step is to accept Jesus as Lord; then as you grow, and revelation is given to you, you will put away earthly or worldly things; which are strife, jealousy, bitterness, etc.

> *"Once you were less than nothing; now you are God's own. Once you knew very little of God's kindness; now your very lives have been changed by it." [I Peter 2:9, The Living Bible]*

Life without Jesus has no real purpose, as there is not anything to hold on to. Once we are changed by the grace of God, though, we not only have a purpose and a reason to live for today, but we also have the hope of our eternal existence with Jesus Christ when He comes after His church.

Chapter 2

THE CARNAL MAN

The carnal man is born again.....he is not necessarily a new born Christian, but he is still a baby in the things of God. The carnal man has accepted Jesus into his life, but has made no real effort to develop and mature into spiritual things. He chooses to be fed with milk instead of meat. You could say he is still ruled by his flesh, rather than putting his trust daily in the things of God. I have said that newborn Christians should be helped, directed, loved, and encouraged by other believers. The time comes, though, when he has to begin taking steps of his own. Just as my wife Sharon took the bottle from our four children, new Christians have to be broken from total dependance on other believers and the Pastor.

Abraham and Sarah had a feast on the day that Isaac was weaned and put on solid food. It was a time to celebrate. (Genesis 21:8) It should be the same way

7

with Christians as they begin to grow and are no longer controlled by their fleshly desires. They learn to walk by faith and not by sight, (II Corinthians 5:7). It's time to celebrate, because they are putting the old things behind and are learning to live victoriously.

The carnal man who is born again may even speak in tongues occasionally, but he is still acting in many ways like the man who is not born again. He has not renewed his mind to the things of God. He is touchy, depressed, and discouraged more than he is encouraged; and he does not experience the prosperity that God has for him.

> *"However, brethren, I could not talk to you as spiritual (men) but as to non-spiritual (men of the flesh, in whom the carnal nature predominates), as to mere infants (in the new life) in Christ—unable to talk yet!*
> *2, I fed you with milk, not solid food, for you were not yet strong enough (to be ready for it); but even yet you are not yet strong enough (to be ready for it),*
> *3, For you are still (unspiritual, having the nature) of the flesh under control of ordinary impulses. For as long as (there are) envying and jealousy and wrangling and factions among you, are you not unspiritual and of the flesh, behaving yourselves after a human standard and like mere (unchanged) men." [I Corinthians 3:1-3, Amplified]*

Notice that Paul addressed the carnal person as brethren. He said that he could not talk to them like spiritual adults, but he had to talk to them as if they

8

were babies in the Christian life, who followed not after the things of God but after their own fleshy desires. Paul told them that they were acting like people who didn't belong to the Lord at all. When you are jealous of one another, and you are competing against each other, wanting your own way, quarreling, and finding fault; it really shows at what stage of growth you are. One may say, "I am a follower of Paul," another says, "I am a follower of Apollos;" this again reveals they are living as ordinary (mere) men.

WHO ARE YOU FOLLOWING?

Carnal Christians are followers of men's personalities more than they are followers of God's character in the men. By doing so, some situations will occur which will cause them to lose confidence in both the man and what the man has shown him from God's Word. On the other hand, the balanced Christian will have confidence in the ones who are used of God, but will not go overboard. They will see that God is in those who are ministering the Word, yet they will go back to the scriptures to see if what they are being told is from God.

"And ye become followers of us, and of the Lord..." [I Thessalonians 1:6]

This is the way it is supposed to be by showing respect, trust, and confidence in the one who is ministering the Word. It is also keeping your eyes on Jesus, who is the author and finisher of your faith.

CARNAL CHRISTIANS ARE CONTROLLED BY THEIR FEELINGS

Some carnal Christians will go to church, but they never apply what is taught to their lives. Some quote and confess the Word and may even seem spiritual; but when attacks from Satan come, they give in to their feelings. They are very touchy, and as a result, cry and feel sorry for themselves. They often say, "I just don't understand why this is happening to me." They become frustrated, discouraged, depressed, and mope around for days.

"Ever learning, and never able to come to the knowledge of the truth." [II Timothy 3:7]

Actually they **know** what to do, but they refuse to take God's Word and do it. Their immaturity shows through any spiritual front that they might have put up. Remember, a carnal Christian is not necessarily a newborn Christian, but is one who at any chronological stage of his Christianity refuses to grow up and develop in the things of God.

EXCUSES

There are some carnal Christians who will use excuses all of the time for not doing the things of God. You may tell them to pray and meditate in the Word, but they have an excuse for not doing so. They have an excuse for not coming to church regularly. They always have a "good" reason to keep from making any real commitment to the body of Christ. A carnal Christian is really unpredictable. One may go to church, one may

10

not; most pretend to be very spiritual. One thing is sure, though; they remain in infancy stages.

SELF-CONTROL

> *"But the fruit of the spirit is love, joy, peace, longsuffering, gentleness, goodness, faith, 23, Meekness, temperance: against such there is no law."* *[Galatians 5:22 & 23]*

The fruit of the spirit is **LOVE**. It is given to you at the new birth; it is imparted to your spirit; it is within your treasure chest; it is deposited into your account to write checks on! You must take self-control and develop the fruit of the spirit every day—in ALL circumstances. **You develop joy, peace, longsuffering, gentleness, goodness, faith, meekness, and temperance**. It is all there in love, but if you don't use self-control and draw the love from within you, you will stay an immature Christian.

You must take responsibility for your actions. You take each day and make it a good one. People will say to you: "Have a nice day." You very seldom just "have" a nice day—you "make it" a nice day. Each day is filled with circumstances; some good and some not so good; so you **must** exercise patience. You must be joyful; you must be kind when you don't feel like it. You must give when you don't feel like it. You must be faithful when you don't feel like it. Make sure that your attitude is the attitude of Jesus in all things.

> *"Be renewed in the attitude of your mind."* *[Ephesians 4:23, paraphrased]*

Some years ago I was invited to speak at a Pentecostal Church. As I began speaking, I noticed a group of people sitting in about the middle of the church. Most of the time they sat with their heads down. When they did look up, however, the expression on their faces were terrible. This went on for sometime. Then all of them got up and walked out. On their way out, one of them spoke out disapprovingly, **"Worldliness!"** I continued to speak as if nothing had happened. After the meeting was over I asked the Pastor, "Do you know the people who walked out?" He said, "Oh yes, they are some of my best members." I then replied, "Apparently I said something that offended them; do you know what it could have been." He told me that it was not anything I had said. I asked, "What, then, was it." He said, "Uh, uh, uh, well, uh, well, it's your hair." At that time my hair was over my ears, and they felt that it was too long. They were calling me worldly, because my hair was over my ears. They were the ones who were worldly, though, because they did not use self-control or show the God-kind of love in their actions. Even if I had been wrong, their immaturity was indicated by the type of attitude they manifested toward me.

Chapter 3

THE SPIRITUAL MAN

"When I was a child, I spake as a child, I understood as a child, I thought as a child: but when I became a man, I put away childish things." [I Corinthians 13:11]

When I was a child, one of my favorite pastimes was pretending with my older brother. We would take a rope and tie one end around our waists, and he would pull me with it. We were pretending to be a tractor and trailer. Even though I enjoyed this, we would normally get into an argument, because I got tired of being the trailer. Sometimes I wanted to be the tractor. My brother normally got his way, though, because he was the oldest. I would also sit in my Dad's car and pretend to drive, or pretend that I was the pilot of an airplane. But I was just a child; I acted and responded like one which was normal. As I began to mature, I put away childish things. I did not pretend any longer; I became of age. I obtained a drivers license and could drive a car.

Paul was saying this same thing; that he was a child. He reasoned and understood as a child until he became a man. At that point he put away childish things. The same is true of the spiritual man. He puts away his old life and walks in the spiritual realm, because he is not controlled by his flesh, but rather by the Spirit of God. Not only are his actions controlled by the Spirit of God, but also his reactions. In emergency situations, or when there is bad news or symptoms, he does not act or react as a carnal Christian would. He stands in the strength of the Word of God and is not moved by the circumstances.

The Word of God has first place in his life; he meditates in the word of God regularly and has a consistent prayer life. As a result of doing this, his thoughts are Godly thoughts; he has the mind of Christ; he walks in Godly wisdom. He knows that he is a winner and that God has made a way of escape for him.

> *"There hath no temptation taken you but such as is common to man: but God is faithful, who will not suffer you to be tempted above that ye are able; but will with the temptation also make a way to escape, that ye may be able to bear it." [I Corinthians 10:13]*

> *"For He hath made Him to be sin for us, who knew no sin; that we might be made the righteousness of God in Him." [II Corinthians 5:21]*

KNOWING YOUR RIGHTEOUSNESS

Truly knowing your righteousness can be the most powerful force in your life. When you know that you are in right standing with God, you know that you have **God's ability!** All fear and inferiority are done away with and have been replaced with the confidence and boldness to do God's will, to live as Jesus lived, and to manifest the greater works in your life that He did! You **cannot** "earn" righteousness...**IT IS YOUR GIFT!**

The spiritual man has accepted this great truth that righteousness is not limited, because it is God's and not man's. You will never run short of His righteousness. You will never be more righteous than you were the moment you were born again, because righteousness does not depend upon your works. However, you **do** grow in the knowledge of what righteousness means to you and how it affects your life. You will see yourself as God sees you — free from your past....all sin removed....**no more guilt or condemnation.**

"Beloved, now are we the sons of God...." [I John 3:2]

Your speech and appearance is like a son. You're not sad, depressed, or defeated. Instead, you have a smile upon your face; your shoulders are held high; you walk the victory walk; and you talk the victory talk. Your prayers are answered because you come to Him with boldness and confidence; you know that you are worthy because of what Jesus did for you at Calvary. You no longer confess, "I am an old sinner saved by grace"

-BUT RATHER, "I was a sinner, but now I am saved and set free from my past by the grace of God!" I have the freedom, ability, confidence, and boldness to enter into the Throne Room of God and fellowship with Him.

> *"Let us therefore come boldly into the throne of grace, that we may obtain mercy, and find grace to help in time of need." [Hebrews 4:16]*

PEACE AND JOY IN THE HOLY GHOST

The spiritual man knows his righteousness, knows that he is in right standing with God, and knows that serving God is more than just going to heaven after physical death. Please don't misunderstand me, I don't want to play down going to heaven or its importance. Going to heaven is a very good reason for serving God, but it should not be the only reason you have for being a Christian. I believe in heaven and actually wait with great anticipation for that great day when I get to go! Life in itself is pretty much a bum ride because of Adam's sin in the garden. It is because of Jesus dying on the cross at Calvary that it is worth living. The spiritual man has this revelation, and he gets more out of serving God. It's as if he has an insurance policy guaranteeing him passage to heaven when he dies, yet he knows that the richness of faithfully serving God here on earth will bring even greater joy when he arrives there.

> *"For the kingdom of God is not meat and drink; but righteousness, peace, and joy in the Holy Ghost." [Romans 14:17]*

The spiritual man knows that walking and living the Christian life by faith is not a struggle, it is peace and joy in the Holy Ghost. It is not hard to serve God when you let Him become **Lord** of your life. Every day is a victory! You always have the hope of heaven and look forward to being reunited with your loved ones in the presence of Jesus forever. Knowing that you will never have to be separated from your loved ones again is such a glorious thought. Right now, though, it is a joy to know the Lord is my shepherd and that I shall neither want nor lack. It is a joy to know the Lord directs my path daily to still waters and to safety; that His presence is with me, anointing me, and will give me goodness and mercy **now**.

MORE THAN A CONQUEROR

The Christian life is not merely waiting and existing until the coming of the Lord. It is with power and confidence that the believer is an example to the unbeliever. He is an imitator of Christ.

"Therefore be imitators of God - copy Him and follow His example - as well-beloved children (imitate their father)." [Ephesians 5:1, Amplified]

He walks the walk that Jesus commanded him to. He takes every opportunity to boldly declare Jesus to his generation and be a witness for Christ anywhere he may be whether in his neighborhood, community, place of business, bus, or telephone. The power of Christ is revealed to the lost and hurting.

"But you shall receive power - ability, efficiency and might - when the Holy Spirit has come upon you; and you shall be My witnesses in Jerusalem and all Judea and Samaria and to the ends - the very bounds - of the earth." [Acts 1:8, Amplified]

The spiritual adult **has no fear.** He is not intimidated by people, because he has God's ability at work in him. God's might and power are within him to witness and take control of inferiority and fear.

"Now we have not received the spirit (that belongs to) the world, but the (Holy) Spirit Who is from God, (given to us) that we might realize and comprehend and appreciate the gifts (of divine favor and blessing so freely and lavishly) bestowed on us by God." [I Corinthians 2:12, Amplified]

The spiritual man is no longer of the world, but he is of God. His desire is the desire of the Holy Spirit, and that desire is to be a conqueror! Not to just barely get by and make it - BUT TO WIN - and bring many other people into the kingdom of God in the process.

"Nay, in all these things we are more than conquerors through Him that loved us.
38, For I am persuaded, that neither death, nor life, nor angels, nor principalities, nor powers, nor things present, nor things to come,
39, Nor height, nor depth, nor any other creature, shall be able to separate us from the love of God, which is in Christ Jesus our Lord." [Romans 8:37-39]

18

The spiritual man obeys the commandment given to him by Jesus in Mark 16:17 & 18. He casts out devils and lays hands on the sick; signs and wonders follow his life. He conquers all circumstances and, with patience, runs the course that is set before him.

THE FIVE MINISTRY GIFTS

"And His gifts were [varied; He Himself appointed and gave men to us,] some to be apostles (special messengers), some prophets (inspired preachers and expounders), some evangelists (preachers of the gospel or traveling missionaries), some pastors (shepherds of His flock), and teachers.

12, His intention was the perfecting and full equipping of the saints, (His consecrated people), [that they should do] the work of the ministering toward building up Christ's body (the church),

13, [That it might develop] until we all attain oneness in the faith and in the comprehension of the full and accurate knowledge of the Son of God; that [we might arrive] at really mature manhood - the completeness of personality which is nothing less than the standard height of Christ's own perfection - the measure of the stature of the fullness of the Christ, and the completeness found in Him.

14, So then, we may no longer be children, tossed; [like ships] to and fro between chance gusts of teaching, and wavering with every changing wind of doctrine, [the prey of] the cunning and

19

cleverness of unscrupulous men, (gamblers engaged) in every shifting form of trickery in inventing errors to mislead.
15, Rather, let our lives lovingly express truth in all things - speaking truly, dealing truly, living truly. Enfolded in love, let us grow up in every way and in all things into Him, Who is the Head [even] Christ, the Messiah, the Anointed One.
16, For because of Him the whole body (the church, in all its various parts closely) joined and firmly knit together by the joints and ligaments with which it is supplied, when each part [with power adapted to its need] is working properly (in all its functions), grows to full maturity, building itself up in love." [Ephesians 4:11-16, Amplified]

The spiritual man understands his need for the five ministries: the apostle, prophet, evangelist, pastor, and teacher. They are given to the body of Christ by God to teach the uncompromised truth so that it will develop to full maturity. The Christian, through the instruction that is received, will do more than come to church. He will do the work of the ministry, building up the members of the body of Christ. The five ministries which are given are all needed; they are all important to bring about the maturity needed. It takes all five of the ministries to give the Christian a proper balance. He cannot be under the teaching of just one of the special gifts. If he accepts only one, he will never be able to develop fully.

When the five ministries and their teaching are

received, the Christian grows out of the childhood stages and matures as he applies the Word of God to his life. The result is love for and the desire to help other members of the body of Christ. Competition is eliminated because everyone works toward the common goals of bringing the entire world to the knowledge of the truth that Jesus Christ is Lord. They no longer chase after or are fooled by false doctrines because of the strong foundations under them. When something is done or taught and their spirit does not bear witness with it, they do not fall or get confused because they stand on the apostles doctrine with Jesus Christ being the chief cornerstone. [Ephesians 2:20]

Every mature Christian has accepted the gift of the pastor. The pastor loves, guides, and gives to his flock. He feeds them, and protects them, and watches for wolves. He also shares his pulpit with the other four ministry gifts, making sure that all get a balanced diet of the Word of God. If you don't have a pastor like this, you should find one. It is **essential** to your spiritual growth.

These first few chapters have given you brief yet concise descriptions of the natural man, the carnal man, and the spiritual man; who they are and what they do. It is my intention in the following chapters to show you how to begin developing spiritual maturity for yourself.

Chapter 4

RENEW YOUR MIND

"I beseech you therefore, brethren, by the mercies of God, that ye present your bodies a living sacrifice, holy, acceptable unto God, which is your reasonable service.
2, And be not conformed to this world: but be ye transformed by the renewing of your mind, that ye may prove what is that good, and acceptable, and perfect, will of God." [Romans 12:1 & 2]

Notice that Paul said, "I beseech you therefore, brethren." This lets you know that he was talking to the Christians. After you have exercised your will to accept Jesus into your life and become born again, you have a further responsibility if you want to do God's will. That responsibility is to give all that you are to God. He said not to be tied to or entangled with the world, but to be renewed in your thinking.

MAN IS A TRIUNE BEING

I Thessalonians 5:13 says that man is a spirit, he has a soul, and he lives in a body. The spirit of man is where the life of God dwells after the New Birth. The change in the spirit is instantaneous. The reign of death under the rule of Satan is transformed, in the twinkling of an eye, into the vibrant life of God. Through the wooing of the Holy Spirit the mind gains the capacity to change and accept Jesus. The spirit does not have this capability.

The soul of man is comprised of the mind, will, and emotions. The change that takes place there is a gradual and progressive one. The soul is so closely associated with the spirit that you cannot always tell where one ends and the other begins. The only sure way to differentiate between the spirit and the soul is through the Word of God.

> *"For the word of God is quick, and powerful, and sharper than any two edged sword, piercing even to the dividing asunder of the soul and spirit..." [Hebrews 4:12]*

The Word of God is alive, powerful, and able to separate the two. The spirit and the soul work together. It takes the constant transformation of the mind through the Word of God to draw out and utilize the fullness of God within man's spirit. If you, after being born again, do not put something into your mind concerning the new life within you, it will revert back to the way it was prior to the New Birth. The patterns of

24

the old man will regain the ascendancy, because the mind has nothing else to draw from except prior experience to make judgments and decisions.

Man lives in a body. His body is his earth suit. The body is not the real person though; it is only the residence of the real person. It functions through the five senses: seeing, hearing, tasting, smelling, and feeling. As has been mentioned before, the man who is not born again is not alive unto God. Consequently, he is controlled by those five senses. The body, by housing the born again spirit and soul depart from the earthly body. The body, having fulfilled its purpose, begins to decay.

The born again man must be a triune being. The spirit, soul, and body must function together to have any effect at all. No one part of that trinity is effective without the other. The born again spirit, if left untapped, is useless. The unrenewed mind cannot draw from the limitless potential of God's life within the spirit. Neither the spirit nor the soul can have any effect unless channeled through the body. They must all function together to fulfill God's ultimate intention for man.

THE SPIRIT OF MAN

"For what man knoweth the things of man, save the spirit of man which is in him? Even so the things of God knoweth no man, but the Spirit of God.

12, Now we have received, not the spirit of the world, but the spirit which is of God; that we might know the things that are freely given to us of God." [I Corinthians 2:11 & 12]

If you have been born again, you have received Him into your spirit. Paul said that you have not received the spirit of the world but the Spirit of God that you might know the things that are freely given to you of God.

"And you hath he quickened, who were dead in trespasses and sins." [Ephesians 2:11]

God's Spirit is united with man's spirit—he is made alive unto God. Man receives God's very nature within him, the nature that knows no bounds. The Bible says that the kingdom of God is within you. [Luke 17:21] It also states in Romans 14:17, that the kingdom of God is righteousness, peace, and joy in the Holy Ghost. The word **kingdom** in both of these verses of scripture is translated from the Greek word basileia, which means rule, reign; (a foundation of power). As a born again Christian, you have received power to rule and reign over Satan in your spirit. Your spirit is actually a *foundation of power here on earth!*

"And ye are complete in Him which is the head of all principality and power:" [Colossians 2:10]

I personally believe that you are complete. It is the same as your body in infancy. All of the organs are there, but they must develop fully to attain maximum capacity. You must also be taught how to develop toward maturity in the area of the soul or thinking realm. Your spirit is truly the king; your soul is the servant; and your body is the slave. Your spirit, though, cannot rule in your life until your mind has been developed and renewed to the things of God.

THE SOUL OF MAN

The soul has much to do with your Christian walk. There are differing opinions about spiritual growth. Some say that it occurs in the spirit of man, but I believe and teach that the real development takes place in the area of the soul. The goal is for your will to become God's will; for your mind to become God's mind; for your emotions to respond to situations as God would. The soul can only become a servant to the spirit as it develops, surrenders, submits or commits to the spirit. Your will decides which is in control, *your spirit - or your emotions.* Many Christians are totally controlled by their emotions, because they have never learned how to control them. Some have been taught, but have chosen to live a negative, defeated life rather than a victorious one.

"Ever learning, and never able to come to the knowledge of the truth." [II Timothy 3:7]

It's difficult for me to understand how people that know the truth will not do what they know to do to be an overcomer. I have not overcome obstacles that have faced me because I am a pastor. I am victorious, because I am an heir of God and a joint heir with Jesus. I want to be happy: so when obstacles come, I think the thoughts of God and I talk the talk of God. Many times in my life I have had the opportunity to be down, discouraged, and feel sorry for myself, but I chose to let the Spirit of God be in control instead of my emotions.

Looking at and talking about the circumstances will make you feel sad and depressed, but looking at God's Word and talking God's Word will change your feelings.

CONTROL YOUR THOUGHTS

"Finally, brethren, whatsoever things are true, whatsoever things are honest, whatsoever things are just, whatsoever things are pure, whatsoever things are lovely, whatsoever things are of good report; if there be any virtue, and if there be any praise, think on these things.
9, Those things, which ye have both learned, and received, and heard, and seen in me, do: And the God of peace shall be with you."
[Philippians 4: 8 & 9]

The child of God must take control of his thoughts. Paul said to think thoughts that are good. Why? Because God is good.

"Every good gift and every perfect gift is from above, and cometh down from the father of lights..." [James 1:17]

When you think of things that are pure, lovely, of good report, etc., you allow the virtue that is in your spirit to flow freely in your mind. Paul told those around him to do the things which they heard and saw in him. He was saying that they had seen him face opposition, pain, and many other problems; but they saw that he *always* thought the thoughts of God and took positive steps. He praised God instead of giving into his feelings!

One good example is when he and Silas were put in jail after having been beaten for preaching the gospel. They did not sit around and have a "pity party", making all kinds of negative statements such as, "I wonder why God let this happen to us when we've been casting out devils, healing the sick, preaching the gospel?" *NO!* They did the very opposite! They sang praises at midnight, an earthquake came and the prison doors flew open. The result of these praises was their freedom and, even better, the jailer received Jesus as Savior. [Acts 16:25-31] They chose to think on the good things rather than the bad, and by doing so, God moved for them.

Right now, take control of your thoughts; think good thoughts; don't let Satan destroy your day.

"This is the day which the Lord hath made, we will rejoice and be glad in it." [Psalm 118:24]

Choose the thoughts that you think on. You have a will; you have a right to do so. Whomever you give your will to is whom you are a servant to.

"Know ye not, that to whom ye yield yourselves servants to obey, his servants ye are to whom ye obey;..." [Romans 6:16]

Whatever you do with the thoughts that enter your mind will determine how you live your life. Every thought must be dealt with individually. One can come from what is stored in your mind, or what is happening around you, be it from God or Satan.

"For the weapons of our warfare are not carnal, but mighty through God to the pulling down of strongholds;
5, Casting down imaginations, and every high

29

> *thing that exalteth itself against the knowledge of God, and bringing in to captivity every thought to the obedience of Christ." [II Corinthians 10:4 & 5]*

There are three words which I would like to point out to you in these two verses of scripture: thoughts, imaginations, and strongholds. A thought, whether it be from God or the devil, will turn into an imagination if you hold on to it. It then progresses into a stronghold. If the thought, imagination, and stronghold is from God—*good;* nothing from Satan can interfere. You will be victorious, because your mind is locked-in to your spirit. Your body will then follow through; as it obeys what is being sent to it through the mind, and the mind is under control of the spirit.

Let me tell you what to do if the thought is either from the devil or a negative thought. Cast it down with prayer or singing praises unto God. Don't let that evil or bad thought turn into an imagination (fear, worry, or unbelief). If it does, you are headed for the next step, a **stronghold**. Satan then has you thinking what he wants you to think, and, consequently, you live a very defeated life.

Satan may put thoughts of evil in your mind, but that does not mean you have sinned. It becomes sin when you refuse to deal with those thoughts and allow them to develop. You might say that when you dwell on a thought it changes ownership, it becomes yours, and you become obedient to it. Satan cannot read your mind. I know that may surprise you, but it is true. He may give you a thought, but you have the opportunity to either reject or entertain it. He does not know whether you are thinking on it or not until you speak about it or act on it.

"If ye then be risen with Christ, seek those things which are above, where Christ sitteth on the right hand of God.
2, Set your affections on things above, not on things on the earth.
3, For ye are dead, and your life is hid with Christ in God." [Colossians 3:1-3]

Paul said to think and seek the things of God, not the things of the world. Don't sit around and worry. Your old life is gone; you now have the life of God and are hid in Christ when you are obedient to Him. Realize that Satan does not know everything. If he knew everything, he would have known exactly where Jesus was and who He was at birth. He would not have killed all the babies in Bethlehem that were two years and under. [Matthew 2:16] Jesus would not have been crucified either.

"Which none of the princes of this world knew: for had they known it, they would not have crucified the Lord of Glory." [I Corinthians 2:8]

The more that you renew your mind to the things of God, the more you will think like God. You will then be able to recognize where every thought comes from.

THE BODY

"What? Know ye not that your body is the temple of the Holy Ghost which is in you, which ye have of God, and ye are not your

own?

20, For ye are bought with a price: therefore glorify God in your body and in your spirit, which are God's." [I Corinthians 6:19 & 20]

When you are born again, your body is the place where God dwells here on earth. As your mind is renewed to the Lord, your body should no longer control you. Before the new birth, man is controlled by his senses—what he sees, feels, etc. As the believer meditates and renews his thinking, his mind begins to store new information. When, at some time, his body sends a message of possibly a disease symptom to his brain, he will begin to exercise the self-control which he has developed by the Spirit of God. Then, instead of allowing his body to rule him, he will rule his body.

On Sunday morning your body will sometimes tell you to stay home and have bedside assembly. "It's alright", your body says, "You need the rest." Or, "You don't need to pray an hour every day." You may make the commitment to pray; but when you begin, your body will try to sleep. Make it obey you. When you start meditating in the Word, your body will again try to rule you. You have God's power. Direct your mind to thinking the thoughts of God; and when you renew your mind every day, you are able to hear the voice of your spirit. When you make the decision to follow that voice, your body will follow suit.

I have said earlier that while you are under the direction of your bodily desires, your spirit is unable to make the decisions. When your will becomes the will of the Spirit, then your spirit takes control. It is king; your soul is the servant; and your body is a slave to your soul. Don't let your body be king. Exercise temperance (self-control). When you give in to your body, you are unable to accomplish God's desire for your life. If you are falling short in the area of appetite, make the quality decision to push that plate back! Going on a diet is not the answer. Self-control is the answer. Do everything you do with moderation at all times.

I have found that I must discipline myself each day, not just when I feel like it. I hardly ever "feel" like it! I am like most people, I love to eat. I eat to live, though, rather than live to eat. I watch what I put in my mouth, as well as the time that it goes in. I do eat some sweets, but *only* in moderation. The secret is moderation. Literally millions of dollars are spent on diets each year, or something that you do to lose weight more quickly. You may lose it rapidly, but the problem lies in keeping that weight off and more from coming back. This is why I personally don't believe in dieting. I believe that you should learn self-control. If you are overweight, decide what you are going to do about it—and do it! Make sure that it is not an "overnight remedy." Take responsiblity for bringing your body under control.

I have a very good friend who had been overweight for several years. He is a professional person and knew that his weight was a hindrance to both his job and his testimony for Christ. He decided to do something about it, and lost 90 pounds over a period of 14 months. He knew that if he had tried to lose it in 2 or 3 months, it would not last. He began to exercise self-control. He ate less than usual each time he sat down to a meal and watched the kinds of food that he ate. He is proud of his accomplishment, because he did not let his flesh win! My referring to anyone with a weight problem is not meant to condemn. It is, however, important for you to make the quality decision to be spirit-controlled. And to be spirit-controlled, you must have self control.

If you smoke cigarettes, it is not good for your health. It is destroying your body. Surely, you are not going to let that little white and brown "coffin nail" rule you. When your mind begins rationalizing the need for one, take the scriptures, memorize, and confess them. Pray in the spirit, sing praises, and call someone to have them agree with you. God has given you power over **all things** to be able to rule and reign in this life.

> *"For if by one man's offense, death reigned by one; much more they which receive abundance of grace and of the gift of righteousness shall reign in life by one, Christ Jesus." [Romans 5:17]*

God has given you the power to be victorious every day in your life, but you are the only one who can exercise your authority. I have used overeating and smoking as only two of the areas in which self control is needed. There are many others, but it seems as if, in my experience, that these are the most common ones.

Growing into maturity by renewing your mind is perpetual. There is no such thing as staying in one place. You either progress or regress. Paul said, "But this one thing I do, forgetting those things which are behind, and reaching forth unto those things which are before, I press toward the mark for the prize of the high calling of God in Christ Jesus." [Philippians 3:13, paraphrased] Every day I have a goal, something I want to achieve. I know that I must press and push forward to obtain it. A winner never quits, and a quitter never wins. Obstacles are there, but I am a winner! You can be too!

Chapter 5

THE POWER OF WORDS

"Death and life are in the power of the tongue: and they that love it shall eat the fruit thereof." [Proverbs 18:21]

The words that you speak over your life are so important. They can set you free, or they can place you in bondage. You bring life or death to yourself by your conversation. When most people receive Jesus into their heart, they must learn how to talk in a new way. A new way is necessary; the old way which was filled with negative words produced sorrow and unhappiness. It hurts me to hear Spirit-filled Christians talking in the negative realm. By doing so you can never actually mature or develop. You will never rise above the level of your confession.

GOD USED WORDS TO CREATE

As much as God used words to create the heavens,

the earth, and man, you use the power in words to create good or bad in your life. Words control your future. Many things have happened to you, both good and bad, because of what you have said. Begin to take inventory of your life right now; examine your conversation to determine whether you are speaking and responding as Jesus would in any given situation. Do you have "weeds" or "flowers" in the garden of your life?

*3, "**And God said,** Let there be light: and there was light.*

*6, **And God said,** Let there be a firmament in the midst of the waters, and let it divide the waters from the waters.*

*9, **And God said,** Let the waters under the heaven be gathered together unto one place, and let dry land appear: and it was so.*

*11, **And God said,** Let the earth bring forth grass, the herb yielding seed, and the fruit tree yielding fruit after his kind, whose seed is in itself, upon the earth: and it was so.*

*14, **And God said,** Let there be lights in the firmament of the heaven to divide the day from the night; and let them be for signs, and for seasons, and for days, and years.*

*20, **And God said,** Let the waters bring forth abundantly the moving creature that hath life, and fowl that may fly above the earth in the open firmament of heaven.*

*26, **And God said,** Let us make man in our image, after our likeness: and let them have dominion over the fish of the sea, and over the fowl of the air, and over the cattle, and over all the* *earth, and over every creeping thir creepeth upon the earth." [G 1:3, 6, 9, 11, 14, 20, 26]*

You *must* come to the understanding that there *is* power in your words. Listed above are seven scriptures in the first chapter of Genesis which declare, "God said." He actually had to say it before it came into being.

"...And the Spirit of God moved upon the face of the water." [Genesis 1:2] The Spirit was with or upon the words that God was speaking, or there could have been no creation. The Spirit of God carried out what He spoke. In the same way God spoke, we speak "words" to receive the life of Christ as a new creation.

I would also like to make you aware here that it takes belief in the creative power of your words.

"That if thou shalt confess with thy mouth the Lord Jesus, and shalt believe in thine heart that God hath raised him from the dead, thou shalt be saved.
10, For with the heart man believeth unto righteousness; and with the mouth confession is made unto salvation." [Romans 10:9 & 10]

There have been some that have said that if you speak something long enough, it will happen. There is some truth to that statement, but there must be some qualification of it.

What actually happens is that when you begin to speak, whether by the Word of God, or by Satan, you give one (God or Satan) the right to bring to pass what is said. Charles Capps said, "God's Word that is conceived in your heart, then formed by the tongue, and spoken out of your own mouth; becomes a spiritual force, releasing the ability of God within you." In other words, when you believe God's Word [in your heart], then speak it forth, you *will* see results! Believe and then speak.

> "...*I believed, and therefore have I spoken; we also believe, and therefore speak;*" *[II Corinthians 4:13]*

When you believe God's Word and it is conceived in your heart, you have understanding. Then, as you speak, you release the force of the Holy Spirit within you to bring what has been spoken into existence.

The same thing happens in the negative realm. When you begin to make statements which are the opposite of what God has said about you in His Word, you begin to believe them. Then Satan, being the god of this world, takes the words which are being spoken from *your* mouth and causes the very things which you are saying to come to pass in your life. You give or deny Satan the power to do evil in your life by what you are speaking.

KEEP YOUR CONVERSATION RIGHT

> "*Whoso offereth praise glorifieth me: and to him that ordereth his conversation aright will I shew the salvation of God.*" *[Psalm 50:23]* The child of God must speak in agreement with the Word of God rather than what the circumstances dictate. Learn the importance of speaking what you want rather than what you don't

Power

40

want. Order your conversation aright **today**, and you will see the glory of God manifested in your life. Paul said to change your conversation from your past life.

> *"That ye put off concerning the former conversation the old man,..."* [Ephesians 4:22]

Every word that a Christian speaks should both edify himself and those who are around him. I don't expect this to happen overnight, but it is very important to your growth and development for you to put this into practice. If you don't change your conversation, you haven't changed your thinking.

> *"Let no man despise thy youth; but be thou an example of the believers, in word, in conversation, in charity, in spirit, in faith, in purity."* [I Timothy 4:12]

He was telling Timothy that people watched and listened to him even in his normal conversation. You, too, should be an example that reveals Christ; not only when you minister publicly, but also in day-to-day life.

If you are a business person, the way in which you talk with people is very important. Not only can you be a success by the words which you speak, but you can also reveal Christ to others by your speech. If you are a secretary, laborer, etc., your words can be very effective to those around you. Always speak positive, encouraging words; words of praise that lift up those around you.

> *"Let the redeemed of the Lord say so;..."* [Psalm 107:2]

IDLE WORDS

"But I say unto you, That every idle word that

41

> men shall speak, they shall give account
> thereof in the day of judgment." [Matthew
> 12:36]

Idle words are nonproductive words, words that have
no life. You will be judged by your words in this life and
at the coming day of judgment. Knowing this, it is
necessary for a child of God to develop the kind of
vocabulary which builds a productive life.

> "He that keepeth his mouth keepeth his life:
> but he that openeth wide his lips shall have
> destruction." [Proverbs 13:13]

When you keep your words in agreement with God's
Word, they produce health, happiness, and more; not
only for yourself, but also for others around you. You
will lift them up and cause them to feel better.

> "Heaviness in the heart of a man maketh it
> stoop: but a good word maketh it glad." [Pro-
> verbs 12:25]

> "A soft answer turneth away wrath: but
> grievous words stir up anger." [Proverbs 15:1]

You may not "feel" like saying good words or giving a
soft answer, but Proverbs says that a good word
maketh the heart glad and that a soft answer will turn
away anger. As you are made aware of who you are in
Christ, it is your responsibility to rid yourself of
negative words.

Your words reveal where you are spiritually to
others. A person may speak evil of someone else. The
one who is spoken against is sometimes quick to
retaliate with the same type of words, because he gives
in to his emotions. *It has been said that if I respond to*

you in the same manner which you have spoken to me, I have given you the power over me to make me in your image. That is no different from the way you acted in the world. Change from the former man; learn to hold your peace.

> "*Even a fool, when he holdeth his peace, is counted wise: and he that shutteth his lips is esteemed a man of understanding.*" [Proverbs 17:28]

It is pretty hard not to say anything if you are spoken against. Contrary to what you may want to do, though, the Word of God says that you are wise if you keep your mouth closed. I believe that one reason why people never reach their full potential in life is a poor attitude that is verbalized. On your job there are negative comments that can be said about the company by a person. If someone else joins in, and then another, little-by-little you may find yourself finding fault with the company also. Don't let yourself get caught in that type of trap. Keep this policy: If you can't say positive things about the company which you work for, then don't say anything at all. You won't regret it.

I've heard people say that they dread going to work. Those words only make matters worse. People will say that they don't like their job, the people they work for, or the people they work with. Once again, they have let their tongue cause negative things to come to them. They made the commitment to the job. If you fit somewhere in these categories, change your attitude and find the things you like about it. Begin to talk about the things which you do like rather than what you don't. Speak good words over your employer.

Don't go around complaining about the working conditions or the pay anymore. Improve the conditions by having a good report to give to other employees and superiors. It won't be long until you are promoted and make more money, because you are sowing good seeds. You should be speaking unity and production rather than division and destruction.

People with good attitudes are noticed on the job by their superiors. They are the ones who get along with others, do their job well, and do not complain. They also speak positive things about their jobs. However, if something is wrong and they are mistreated on the job, there are proper steps to take in correcting the situations. Complaining to other employees or siding with those who complain causes even more strife. Superiors also notice those who needlessly cause strife and give them ample opportunity to complain, usually from outside the employment of that company.

DON'T BE A GOSSIP

As you begin to mature in the things of God, you speak more like a child of God than a child of darkness. Your speech reveals Jesus Christ. There has been much harm done within the body of Christ because of the following. Someone makes a mistake. Another immature or carnal Christian tells others of that mistake. They tell others, and so on and on until that person's reputation is severely damaged. Most of the time, when a person falls or makes a mistake, they are sorry and suffer enough for the wrong they have done. Why should other Christians make it worse for them? I once heard it said that the Christian army is the only one which buries its wounded. In many instances this is true. I admonish you to consider carefully in prayer what you are doing is you are repeating wrongs that others have made and have had enough confidence in you to share them with you.

"He that covereth a transgression seeketh love; but he that reporteth a matter separateth very friends." [Proverbs 17:9]

When you see a person make a mistake, talk to them; not someone else. Go directly to God and pray for them. James said that your tongue is full of deadly poison. False reports that have been spoken have brought a lot of harm and wounds to many good people.

"A tale bearer revealeth secrets: but he that is of a faithful spirit concealeth the matter." [Proverbs 11:13]

"The words of a tale bearer are as wounds, and they go down into the intermost parts of the belly." [Proverbs 18:8]

"He that goeth about as a tale bearer revealeth secrets: therefore meddle not with him that flattereth with his lips." [Proverbs 20:19]

"Where no wood is, there the fire goeth out: so where there is no tale bearer, the strife ceaseth.

21, As coals are to burning coals, and wood to fire; so is a contentious man to kindle strife.

22, The words of a tale bearer are as wounds, and they go down into the intermost parts of the belly.

23, Burning lips and a wicked heart are like a potsherd covered with silver dross." [Proverbs 26:20-23]

Many good friends have been separated by a false tongue. Tale bearers have caused churches to be broken apart and split. Ministries have been deeply hurt because of those who have repeated what they've heard. Don't be caught in Satan's snare. Choose to speak and give only good reports. Build up and edify your brothers and sisters in Christ. Don't be caught repeating things that are not edifying and uplifting. Let your words be words of faith; words of life and encouragement. As you speak good over others, they will speak good over you!

SPEAK POSITIVELY
IN BAD CIRCUMSTANCES

One of the things that Sharon and I have learned to do is to always speak positively when the circumstances are bad. We have had some very difficult times in our lives which have caused us much pain. Many times the pain was so bad that we could not hold back the tears, but we chose to speak only life. We would praise the Lord or just pray in tongues. This gave God the opportunity to bring healing and refreshment to us. This can be very important to you also if you will develop a life of praise. I've heard Christians complain by saying, "I don't understand; I've done all I know to do. Why is this happening to me?" I'm not trying to tell you that I haven't had these same thoughts, because I have; but when they came, I would not let them stay in my mind. I would say over and over again, "This is the day the Lord has made; I will rejoice and be glad in it." Refreshment and restoration *always* came.

If you lose your job, don't complain. Speak positive words such as, "The Lord will provide. God has something better for me. The Lord directs my path. He is my helper." Don't give in to your feelings and speak negatively. Satan wants you to say things like, "I don't know what we're going to do," or "We'll probably lose the house, the car, the furniture, and everything we have." *DON'T REPEAT THESE THINGS EVEN THOUGH YOU MAY FEEL LIKE IT!* Remember in times of tests and trials, speak only positive words, words which are in agreement with God's Word. You may be a newborn Christian or someone who already has knowledge of these things, but the important thing is to do what the Word says to do, whether you feel like it or not!

Remember that your words guide or direct you. They have the power to produce life or death. When you speak things which are evil or negative, you are affected both inwardly and outwardly. God's love within you is a vital force, and the love which you give to others brings life to both them and you. If you take the love that is within you and selfishly turn it inward, it will destroy you. That is why I say it is so important to always speak good things.

> *"A man's belly shall be satisfied with the fruit of his mouth; and with the increase of his lips shall he be filled."* [Proverbs 18:20]

You have the choice to either be fulfilled or destroyed by your words. Choose to be fulfilled by the good words that you speak over others and yourself.

I remember one situation that hurt me deeply. When I was an evangelist, I travelled frequently and was away from my home much of the time. I received a call late one afternoon that my daughter, Tammy, had been struck by an automobile and wasn't expected to live through the night. When I arrived at the hospital and saw the extent of the injuries my daughter suffered, my emotions would have had me scream out, "Why me, Lord? What have I done? I've been a faithful servant for years, and what did I do to deserve this?" My emotions were in turmoil, but the foundation of the Word of God rose up within me and I repeated over and over again, with tears streaming down my face, "Father, I love you, I praise You, I thank You for Your love for me." I would also pray in tongues. God strengthened me inwardly by my choosing the proper words.

> *"Behold also the ships, which though they be so great, and are driven of fierce winds, yet are they turned about with a very small helm, whithersoever the governor listeth." [James 3:4]*

James said that the rudder of a ship is small and yet it keeps a big ship on course even in the midst of strong and fierce winds. James compared the rudder of a ship to your tongue. He said in verse 6 that your tongue can defile your entire body and set the course of what your life will be like. Set your course in right direction by the words of your mouth every day.

> *"Let the words of my mouth, and the meditation of my heart, be acceptable in thy sight, O*

48

Lord, my strength, and my redeemer." [Psalms 19:14]

He can only strengthen and help you when your words are acceptable. He cannot accept your words when they are not in agreement with His Words.

"A wholesome tongue is a tree of life: but perverseness therein is a breech in the spirit." [Proverbs 15:4] When you are speaking the right words, you are releasing God's power; but when you begin talking and saying words contrary to God's Word, they bring bruising, hurt, and brokenness in the spirit. It actually grieves the heart of God when you do not control your words. I know that most people say bad things, because they have not been taught differently. They are saying the things which they have heard all of their life, and sadly many have heard their spiritual leaders say these same things in their presence.

DON'T BE A STUMBLING BLOCK

There are those who have become stumbling blocks for people new in the walk of faith, and they seem to fall into two categories: the first being those who have the intellectual knowledge of the power of the Word and want to have the respect of others by virtue of that knowledge; and the second, those who have genuinely received some revelation from the Word concerning confession and want everyone else to be at their level "right now". A descriptive phrase has been coined for them: confession inspectors. Both are overbearing, but for different reasons.

The first type have heard a few (if that many)

messages on "What You Say Is What You Get," and have not found out about basing every promise of God on all of the Bible, not just a few verses and a message. Their language was as negative as anyone else's before they heard about confession, yet they seem to forget that. They have a desire to correct any negative vocabulary in everyone whom they come in contact with. This correction, however, tends to bring condemnation and bondages to words, not freedom. They also try to make confession a law rather than seeing the grace of the Lord. They don't see confession as the outward expression of inward faith and are intolerant of views or beliefs contrary to what they "know." They may speak the truth in some cases, but it is spoken without love or compassion and is comparable to the way in which the Pharisees spoke in Jesus' day.

The second type are those who have had a genuine change in their life. They have truly seen the power in their words and want everyone else to have the same knowledge. They have more zeal than knowledge, though, and are very quick to correct. Many times they cause hurt and embarrassment and do more harm than good. The result is the same as those who only have the intellectual knowledge even though their intentions are honorable.

There is a way to correct people, but there must be a balance. The person who is speaking negatively must be made to understand why he is saying the wrong thing. Pointing out one poor choice of words is not the answer. The remedy lies in gently directing them towards what the Word of God says concerning the situation or circumstace that they are speaking negatively about.

If the person who has some knowledge of proper confession, though, is not thoroughly grounded in what the Word says about it, he should say nothing. The reason is that partial truth can easily lead to confusion and error. The person who is speaking negatively must also have a teachable attitude. If that is not apparent, no revelation will come to him and the truth of the Word will have fallen on deaf ears. When I hear Christians speaking in the negative realm, it hurts me, but I either say nothing or find a way to help them which won't hurt or embarrass them. I do my utmost to speak the truth in love.

JUSTIFIED OR CONDEMNED

"For by thy words thy shalt be justified, and by thy words thou shalt be condemned." [Matthew 12:37]

I believe that your words open the door for Satan to bring things to you. Below I am going to point out some of the things that Christians say. Check yourself to see if any of these are in your vocabulary.

"IF ANYTHING BAD IS GOING TO HAPPEN, IT'LL HAPPEN TO ME. BAD THINGS ALWAYS HAPPEN TO ME."

"I KEEP A COLD ALL WINTER."

"THE KIDS STAY SICK ALL WINTER."

"I GET HEADACHES ALL OF THE TIME."

"I GET HAYFEVER EVERY SPRING."

"IF ANYONE GETS LAID OFF, IT'LL BE ME."

51

"I'LL BE IN DEBT FOREVER."

"IT LOOKS LIKE I'LL NEVER BE ABLE TO PAY ALL MY BILLS."

"WE ARE ALWAYS BEHIND."

"THINGS NEVER GO RIGHT FOR US/ME."

"MY FATHER HAD A HEART ATTACK, I PROBABLY WILL TOO."

"MY MOTHER HAS HIGH BLOOD PRESSURE, I PROBABLY WILL."

"WE ALWAYS HAVE TO DO WITHOUT."

"WE WILL NEVER BE ABLE TO HAVE NICE THINGS."

"WE DON'T EVER GET TO TAKE A VACATION; WE CAN'T AFFORD IT."

"WE'LL ALWAYS BE POOR. WE CAN'T EVER SAVE MONEY BECAUSE SOMETHING ALWAYS HAPPENS."

"WE WILL NEVER ACHIEVE OUR DREAM."

"WE CAN NEVER BUILD OUR NEW HOME."

"WE WILL ALWAYS HAVE TO BUY A USED CAR. WE CAN'T AFFORD A NEW ONE."

"COME TO OUR HOUSE AND SEE HOW POOR FOLKS LIVE."

"WE CAN'T AFFORD STEAK."

"EVERYTHING I EAT TURNS TO FAT."

"I WILL ALWAYS BE BIG AND OVERWEIGHT."

"I WILL PROBABLY GO BALD. MY FATHER

WAS."

"OUR MARRIAGE IS GOING DOWNHILL."

"OUR CHILDREN KEEP GETTING WORSE."

"EVERY TIME I REALLY START PRAYING, SOMETHING GOES BAD."

"EVERY TIME WE GIVE EXTRA TO THE WORK OF THE LORD, SOMETHING ALWAYS HAPPENS."

"I GIVE AND NEVER GET BACK ANYTHING."

"IF I COULD EVER GET OUT OF DEBT ENOUGH TO SEE FIT, I'D PAY MY TITHES."

"NOBODY LIKES ME. I'M NO GOOD TO ANYONE."

This list of what some Christians say could go on and on. What they are doing is opening themselves up to be snared by their words.

> *"Thou art snared with the words of thy mouth, thou art taken with the words of thy mouth."* [Proverbs 6:2]

> *"He that keepeth his mouth keepeth his life: but he that openeth wide his lips shall have destruction."* [Proverbs 13:3]

Statements like those are opposite of what God has said about you. When you make these types of confessions, you bring a snare and destruction upon yourself. Learn to say the right words over yourself, your spouse, and your family. Speak what you want, not what you see.

"Set a watch, O Lord, before my mouth; keep the door of my lips. [Psalm 141:3]

I pray the above scripture every day. I don't want to give Satan any room to bring bad things into my life.

"Neither give place to the devil." [Ephesians 4:27]

If you open your mouth and speak according to what you see, you will give him place and resultant authority over you.

POOR-MOUTH CHRISTIANS

I have talked with many born again Christians who speak negatively about everything. There are several reasons why these people speak lack in their lives, and some of them are: fear of attack by Satan if they speak the blessings of God; false modesty to obtain the sympathy and support of other people; they are trained to do so by traditional teaching; and they are unwilling to use the Word of God to better themselves (laziness).

In every reason expressed there is a common thread; that of a poor self-image. Those who "poor-mouth" do not look at God's righteousess and see nothing but filthy rags. The result is their eventual downfall because the negative speech will be followed by negative actions. A seed truly bears after its own kind.

CREATIVE WORDS

"...my tongue is the pen of a ready writer."
[Psalm 45:11]

The words which you speak should always be words that express what you want to happen; not what you don't want to happen. Jesus was a perfect example of saying what He wanted:

"...*Let us pass over unto the other side.*" [Mark 4:35]

He told His disciples to get into the boat and cross to the other side. In the process He went to sleep. Jesus meant what He said. On the way across a storm came up and the disciples became fearful. It did not alarm Jesus, though, He just "spoke" to the storm, and the waves calmed. He did not change His confession because the storm came. He rebuked the winds and the sea. He didn't start saying things like, "I don't kow what we are going to do!" He spoke creatively. Don't continue speaking things the way they are; call them the way you want them to be.

God told Abraham, "I have made thee a father of many nations." He spoke over Abraham the end result rather than calling out what the situation looked like at the time. Abraham was past age, and Sarah's womb was *dead!* In the natural she could not bear a child. God did not tell Abraham that he was too old, though, or Sarah that her womb was dead. He said, "I have made thee a father." Abraham believed those words that God spoke rather than what he and Sarah could see with their eyes. Sarah had a child because of God's Word. You see, you must speak words of faith and confidence, not words of doubt and unbelief.

David overcame Goliath. When David saw him, he did not think about the size of Goliath. He did not compare his size to the size of Goliath. He instead compared **God's size** to Goliath's size. He did not think Goliath was too big to hit; rather he was too big to miss! David went to Goliath speaking creative words.

> *"Then said David to the Philistine, Thou comest to me with a sword, and with a spear, and with a shield: but I come unto thee in the name of the Lord of Hosts, the God of the armies of Israel, whom thou hast defied.*
>
> *46, This day will the Lord deliver thee into mine hand; and I will smite thee, and take thine head from thee; and I will give the carcasses of the host of the Philistines this day unto the fowls of the air, and to the wild beasts of the earth; that all the earth may know that there is a God in Israel.*
>
> *47, And all this assembly shall know that the Lord saveth not with sword and spear: for the battle is the Lord's, and He will give you into our hands." [I Samuel 17:45-47]*

David did not let the size of the giant cause him to fear. He knew that God was with him. He went towards the giant speaking words of power and destroyed him. You can destroy the giants in your life, too! It takes time to develop, though. Remember, that's what this book is all about, developing into a mature Christian.

DON'T BE DISCOURAGED

People have come and told me they tried speaking things in a positive way and nothing every happened, or they spoke health to their body and got sick anyway. Results do not come because you are saying something, *you must believe it!* Believe first, then say it. Give yourself enough time to get the words and thoughts of God into your thinking. When you do Satan will try you to see if you really believe what you are saying.

You've walked and talked in the negative realm for so long, and you will not change overnight. That is where so many people fail. They start out right but get discouraged after a while, because everything that they speak does not immediately come to pass. If you fail or get sick as you try to do the Word of God, so what! As a child you stumbled and fell, but you always got back up and walked again, didn't you? In school when you took a test and failed, or when you failed a grade, you repeated it until you passed. Why shouldn't it be the same way in any walk that you take? When something goes wrong, get up and start again until you win. The circumstances only get worse if you give up.

Once a man gave me an immature peach tree. He said, "Don, when the tree blooms, pinch off the buds." I said, "What for? I want peaches." He replied, "You can leave them on if you want to, and it will produce peaches the first year. What happens, though, is that all of its energy will be given to the peaches and the tree will never be very strong." He said that if I would pinch off the buds and let the tree grow strong roots and branches, I would always have good peaches. That made a lot of sense to me. You should do the same. Speak God's Word. Give yourself time to lay a foundation under you before you try to operate at the same level of someone who has been walking in the Word for several years. Speak according to your faith, and not someone else's. Take one step at a time, one day at a time. Do all that you know to do today. As it takes time to learn and develop in the natural senses - it is the same in the kingdom of God.

> ..."*The words that I speak unto you, they are spirit, and they are life.*" [John 6:63]

As you mature you will begin to speak by the spirit; and when your words are spirit and life as Jesus' words were, you will see results. You cannot speak out of your emotions, greed, or selfishness and expect circumstances to change. When your desire becomes God's desire, and your life becomes God's life, your result is God's result.

DON'T PRAY THE PROBLEM

> "*Therefore I say unto you, What things soever ye desire, when ye pray, believe that ye receive them, and ye shall have them.*" [Mark 11:24]

Many people have failed to get answers from God because they have gone to Him and told Him how bad the situation was rather than telling Him what they wanted done about the situation. Some women who have unsaved husbands are continually telling God and everyone else how bad he is. If you have an unsaved spouse tell God what you want him/her to be instead of what he/she is. Praying the problem has no effect. Tell God what you desire the situation to be like.

Jesus is your intercessor, and when you pray to God in Jesus' name, you can only pray the things which He can present to the Father. He can only present positive prayers to the Father; therefore your petitions must be positive.

> "...*consider the Apostle and High Priest of our profession, Jesus Christ.*" *[Hebrews 3:1]*

When Jesus was here on earth, He was sent from God to be an Apostle to all men. He finished that work, and is now at the right hand of the Father ever living to make intercession for everyone. He keeps your confession before the Father as long as it is a confession of faith.

> "...*seeing he ever liveth to make intercession for them.*" *[Hebrews 7:25]*

> "*For Christ is not entered into the holy places made with hands, which are figures of the true; but unto heaven itself, now to appear in the presence of God for us.*" *[Hebrews 9:24]*

DON'T GET UNDER BONDAGE

I have found that as I have traveled around as a speaker in different seminars and camp meetings I have met people who need prayer or someone to pray the prayer of agreement with them. They have definite needs but are afraid to tell anyone what the situation is, because they fear a rebuke if a "bad confession" is made!" This is a sad commentary for the walk of love. If you want someone to pray with you, you must tell this person what you want them to pray for so they can be in agreement with you and know how to pray for you.

The word **"agree"** means to be absolutely harmonious as an orchestra would be in complete harmony. The person with whom you desire to be in agreement must care enough to make your situation a priority over what is going on in his/her life at the time. You can't be in agreement until both of you have an understanding. This does not mean, though, that you go around telling everyone how you feel or all of your problems. No; only tell the one whom you want prayer and agreement with.

TWO KINDS OF TRUTH

A person may say, "I'm not going to say that I'm healed when I know that I'm sick." I, in turn, ask the question, "Why not?" This person has not matured to the point of understanding that. There are two kinds of truth. 1) There is physical truth. This is what your body can discern with the five senses. It could be financial problems, unemployment, cancer, deafness, etc. If you are sick, you are sick—BUT you don't have to stay in that condition. There is something better. 2) There is revelation truth. This is what God's Word says about you and the situatios that you are presently in.

> *"Who his own self bare our sins in His own body on the tree, that we, being dead to sins, should live unto righteousness: by whose stripes ye were healed." [I Peter 2:24]*

Notice that the healing in the above scripture is a past action. It is not something that is to happen in the future. If you say you believe that God is going to heal you, you are still putting it in the future. He has already done it! At Calvary, He provided healing for you. As you renew your mind through the Word of God you begin to obtain revelation truth and can say with absolute surety, "I believe that I am healed by the stripes of Jesus."

That revelation truth taps into the life and light of God within your spirit which consumes the darkness of sickness or disease. You are not speaking a lie. You are changing the natural by the supernatural.

"While we look not at the things which are seen, but at the things which are not seen: for the things which are seen are temporal; but the things which are not seen are eternal." [II Corinthians 4:18]

The spirit world is infintely more powerful than the natural world. The things that you see and feel are subject to change.

"For I am the Lord, I change not..."

The power of God is greater than any circumstance. Believe God's Word; speak it rather than what you see or feel.

"...let the weak say, I am strong." [Joel 3:10]

You are not telling a lie when you speak and say what God says. Previously I gave you a number of statements that people say in the negative realm. When they are making those statements nothing has occurred but their belief and consequent confession will bring the nonexistent into existence. Is that telling a lie?

"And base things of the world, and things which are despised, hath God chosen, yea, and things which are not, to bring to nought things that are." [I Corinthians 1:28]

Paul said the situations which you are facing now are

61

changed and brought to nought by the Spirit of God. The things that "are not" change what "is." Instead of believing and speaking the negative, believe and speak God's blessings over your situations.

A young man in my church recently called and said, "Pastor, I want to give you a good report. I have been unemployed for several weeks, but my wife and I have been speaking a good job, a particular job that I wanted. The hope in getting this job was nearly impossible, because the company had laid off people. The fact that I was told there were 6,000 people who wanted the job also tried to discourage us, but I disregarded all the negative. My wife and I spoke and agreed for that job and were not moved by the circumstances. They called me up at 3:30 a.m. in the morning and told me to come to work. He did not tell a lie. The things that "were not" changed the things that "were." Remember, don't keep calling the things that "are" as though they "are," call them as you want them to be.

Once a person was doing some volunteer work in one of my offices. Each time I would go into the room, she would say, "I don't have a runny nose." I asked, "Why do you keep wiping it then?" She was telling a lie; she did have a runny nose. She didn't understand the true meaning of confession. I began to share the Word with her and then had her confess, "I believe that I receive my healing into my body by the stripes of Jesus." Healing had already been provided for her, but it was up to her to believe and receive healing into her body.

Make the words that you speak be words of life.

Have you ever noticed how much death is in your vocabulary? I know that you have heard people say, "That just tickled me to death." I know that it is only a figure of speech, but don't give Satan any room. It sure would sound much better to say, "That tickled me to life." You've heard things such as, "That scared me to death." If you are frightened by a situation, to add to it by your words can do nothing but harm. Put life into your vocabulary. Remember the words that will work for you. Don't say the words that will work against you.

> *"Fight the good fight of faith, lay hold on eternal life, whereunto thou art also called, and hast professed a good profession before many witnesses." [I Timothy 6:12]*

Chapter 6

FORGIVENESS

"And when ye stand praying, forgive, if ye have ought against any: that your Father also which is in heaven may forgive you your trespasses.

26, But if ye do not forgive, neither will your Father which is in heaven forgive your trespasses." [Mark 11:25 & 26]

Learning to forgive is another vital step toward your spiritual growth. As long as you keep unforgiveness in your heart, you **cannot** develop. God cannot forgive you as long as you hold on to unforgiveness, because unforgiveness is a sin that you are presently doing, not one done in the past. Many people ask God to give them the desires in their heart through Mark 11:24 yet ignore the prerequisite of verses 25 & 26. You must forgive those who have offended, hurt, or spoken against you. You must loose or release them from any sin that they have committed against you. Notice that He said to forgive when you pray. He did not tell you to pray for God to forgive them; *He said for YOU to forgive them!*

GO TO YOUR BROTHER

Many people miss it by saying, "I didn't do anything to him; he is the one who treated me badly. Let him come to me, and I will forgive him." Brothers and sisters, this is not what the Bible says to do.

> *"Moreover if thy brother shall trespass against thee, go and tell him his fault between thee and he alone: if he shall hear thee, thou hast gained thy brother.*
>
> *16, But if he will not hear thee, then take with thee one or two more, that in the mouth of two or three witnesses every word may be established.*
>
> *17, And if he shall neglect to hear them, tell it unto the church: but if he neglect to hear the church, let him be unto thee as an heathen man and a publican." [Matthew 18:15-17]*

If your brother in Christ speaks against you and hurts you, go to him first, not someone else in the church. Go to him and make the effort to resolve the issue and forgive him. If he hears you, you have regained him as a brother. If not, go back to him with one or two more, so that in the mouth of two or three witnesses every word will be established. If he still doesn't hear you, then take it to the church; and if he neglects to hear the church, then let him be to you *as a* heathen. Don't let him be a thorn in your side.

HOW MANY TIMES SHOULD I FORGIVE HIM?

"Then came Peter to him, and said, Lord, how oft shall my brother sin against me, and I forgive him? till seven times?

22, Jesus said unto him, I say not unto thee, Until seven times: but, Until seventy times seven." [Matthew 18:21-22]

Here are two verses of scripture where Jesus is showing the responsibility of Christians. He is not saying to forgive 490 times in one day, *but that the power you have to forgive is unlimited! No matter what a person does against you; you can keep forgiving him!* Don't hold a grudge or hard feelings against this person. Jesus has forgiven you, and, in turn, you have the freedom to forgive him.

RELEASE THEM AND YOU'LL BE RELEASED

"...Whatsoever you bind on earth shall be bound in heaven: and whatsoever ye loose on earth shall be loosed in heaven." [Matthew 18:18] Jesus is actually saying here that what you do not forgive on the earth is not forgiven in heaven. Jesus forgave you of your sins; likewise, you are to forgive anyone that hurts you. If you don't forgive them, the very sin that you retain will come back on you!

Have you ever noticed that the son of an alcoholic

father will say, "I will never turn out to be like my father." Time passes on, though, and he becomes an alcoholic. Why? Because he will not forgive his father. The same thing is true with people who have been abused by their parents. Many times they turn out to be child abusers, because they won't forgive the one who abused them. The truth is that when you hold on to unforgiveness, you are hurting yourself. Life is so short; turn loose and live free.

IF YOU DON'T FORGIVE, YOU'LL BE TORMENTED

Jesus spoke more about forgiveness in Matthew 18:23-35. It was in this chapter that a man owed a large sum of money. The King demanded that the debt be paid in full; and if he could not pay it, his wife, his children, and all of his possessions would be sold to pay the debt. The servant fell down and cried for mercy before the King. The King had compassion on him and forgave him; he was freed by the King from the debt!

The servant then left the King and went to a man who owed him very little in comparison to what he had owed the King. The servant took the man who was in debt to him by the throat and told him to pay all that he owed. The debtor fell down at his feet and begged, "Have patience with me, and I will pay you all I owe you." The servant would not wait. He had the debtor thrown in jail until the debt was paid in full.

The debtor had a friend who went to the King and told him what the servant had done after being forgiven of his debt. The King then called the servant whom he had forgiven to him and said, "You evil-hearted wretch! I forgave you of a large debt, because you asked me to. You, likewise, should have had mercy on the person who owed you. I am going to turn you over to the tormentors until you pay everything you owe."

"And his lord was wroth, and delivered him to the tormentors, till he should pay all that was due unto him.

35, So likewise shall my heavenly Father do also unto you, if ye from your hearts forgive not every one his brother their trespasses."
[Matthew 18:34 & 35]

Jesus said that if you do not forgive others for what they have done, you will be turned over to the tormentors. <u>Your life will be one of confusion, strife, and bitterness because of your unforgiving attitude.</u> You will be subject to the torment of Satan until you do.

BITTERNESS

"Let all bitterness, and wrath, and anger, and clamour, and evil speaking, be put away from you, with all malice:

32, And be ye kind one to another, tenderhearted, forgiving one another, even as God for Christ's sake hath forgiven you."
[Ephesians 4:31 & 32]

<u>If you do not forgive, you become bitter.</u> You are driven by bitterness, and everything that you do or say comes out that way. Saul was consumed with bitterness. For his acts of disobedience, he lost his anointing by God to

69

be King of Israel to David. His bitter feelings controlled him, because he would not forgive David, even though David had done no harm to him. He and his army chased David throughout the land intending to kill him. When David killed Goliath with Saul's blessing, the people of Israel praised David's act and infuriated Saul even more. By not dealing with his bitterness by forgiving, Saul's remaining days on earth were spent in unhappiness, strife, and inner-torment. The same thing happens today when people in the ministry (or anywhere) become jealous of each other. Bitterness creeps in as a result, and men of God are set at odds with each other. The work of the Lord is hindered, and Satan takes delight in that. What difference does it really make whom God uses as long as His desire is accomplished?

If you don't forgive others, the bitterness that gets inside is like an infected sore. Until it is dealt with, the situation continually gets worse. You are the one who suffers. You are filled with the effects of bitterness, and God cannot help you. If there has been something that you have been holding on to and haven't forgiven, it is festering up like a sore; you can't cover it up. *FOR YOUR SAKE GET RID OF IT!* I don't care who the person is or what he has done, he is not the one you hurt by holding it inside. You are hurting yourself and making your life miserable.

FORGIVE BY FAITH

Don't say, "I can't forgive." YOU CAN! A very Godly woman from the western part of the United

States had a daughter who attended a Bible College and worked part time. As the daughter was returning home from her job, she was raped, stabbed to death, and her body thrown beside a road. The mother was a widow; her daughter was **all** she had. Now she felt a void, as if she had nothing. As time passed she began to fill that void inside of her with hatred because of the bitterness toward the unknown murderer. She wondered why God had let this happen to her, especially since her daughter was studying to be a missionary. Her friends could no longer enjoy her because of her attitude.

Finally the murderer was caught, and pleaded guilty to the crime. She began to hate even more then, because she now knew who the man was. She thought to herself over and over, "Why should he live when my daughter is dead?" Two years passed, and she was miserable. The bitterness within tormented her day and night. She had no friends and was all alone.

One day as she sat in a Sunday school class the lesson on love and forgiveness pierced that barrier she had built around her. These words began to well up inside her: "Set yourself free from your prison of hate. Forgive, and you will be free." She was so bound by bitterness that she did not know how to begin. Someone told her of Matthew 6:14, which says, "For if you forgive men their trespasses, your heavenly Father will also forgive you." So by faith she made the effort. She purchased some Bibles and sent them to the penitentiary where the murderer was serving his life sentence. She asked that one be delivered personally to the man who murdered her daughter. She sent this message with it: "I forgive you. Jesus said, Love one another as I have loved you." Then she signed her name. As she did so, it was as if a great weight was lifted from her. **She was free!** She had found peace at last, because she forgave him. She also prayed for him to receive Jesus as his Savior.

Several months passed and she heard nothing. One day a phone call came from a friend. "I have a letter to share with you," she said, "It's from the man in prison to whom you sent a Bible, the man who killed your daughter." The man explained in the letter how he had accepted Jesus as his Savior because of the Bible and the message which was sent with it. He went on to say that he had never been given a gift before; and that since she showed him such forgiveness, he had been able to believe that God would do the same for him. His life was totally changed; and he now conducts Bible Studies in the prison. Other inmates have been saved because of his testimony and witness. The woman continues to support him with material, financial aid, and prayer. He has now become the missionary that her daughter had planned to be. When she released him by forgiving him, freedom came to her. Once again, life was worth living.

You may have been hurt emotionally by your spouse, treated wrongly, cheated, lied about, or stripped of everything. No matter what has happened, turn loose of bitterness **now**. You are the only one who will be consumed by it if you don't...not the other person.

FORGIVE AND FORGET

I said in the beginning of this chapter that you are

unable to develop until you forgive. Now you can see more clearly how holding on to past hurts can hinder you and keep you from loving and trusting other people. If you have remarried, and have not forgiven your former spouse, you will never be able to have the kind of marriage you could have if you would turn loose and set yourself free.

A woman may find out that her husband has been unfaithful to her. She decides to stay in the marriage and tells him that she has forgiven him. She continues to be a dutiful wife, but makes life hell on earth for him because she is cold and flaunts her moral "superiority."

She may tell him she loves him but he can't understand why she continues to be so cold towards him. She will say, "Well, I have forgiven you but I haven't forgotten..." This is a thorn in his side. Actually what she is trying to do is make him do penance. She has never truly forgiven him; for if she had, she would not continually dwell on what happened. Forgiveness that is dwelled upon or continually talked about is not true forgiveness. If one keeps reminding the other of what they have forgiven them of, they are only reinfecting the wound. If you are throwing up past wrongs to your spouse, you *have not* forgiven them. In the example that I used here, it could be the other way around and be an unfaithful wife also. Satan doesn't care whom he uses to destroy a marriage.

When you tell someone you will forgive but cannot forget, it is another way of saying you cannot forgive. I know that it is not easy to forget what has happened, but you can renew your mind and think on good or pure thoughts instead of the past. One person said that

73

forgiveness should be like a cancelled note...it should be torn in two and burned so that it can never place anyone in debt again. Forgiveness which is a show, only half hearted or partial, is like an operation done on a person which is never completed—it is actually worse than before. If you feel proud of your forgiveness or remember it too much, you will be very apt to feel that the other person owes you something for forgiving them. Once again there has been no real forgiveness because you have not released him/her.

The one who truly forgives eradicates or cancels the wrong of others as if it had never been done. You become willing to give up the debt with no mental reservations. In true forgiveness you cancel the debt; not because you are a generous person, or you feel as if you are better or morally superior for not making the other person pay for his wrong, but you realize that you have not hated and condemned the person in the first place. When you decide to forgive, you realize there is nothing to forgive.

DON'T CONDEMN

One of the ways to keep from getting hurt in everyday life is to keep your feelings under control. People will say and do things to you as long as you live here on earth but don't condemn them, and there will be nothing to forgive. Separate their sin from them. In dealing with people an old saying has been given: "A peach is not its fuzz, a toad is not its warts, and a person is not his or her sharp comments." Learn to make the distinction, and you will realize that it is Satan trying to destroy you. In John 8, a woman was brought to

74

Jesus by the Scribes and Pharisees who had been caught in the act of adultery. They wanted to stone her, but Jesus said, "He that is without sin among you let him cast the first stone at her." Those who heard him were convicted of their own sin and began to walk away. Jesus said to the woman, "Where are thine accusers? Hath no man condemnest thee?" She said, "No man, Lord." Jesus said, "Neither do I condemn thee." Jesus did not condemn her, so He did not have to forgive. You learn a valuable lesson when you see the influence of Satan in what a person may say or do to you that would tend to hurt. You do not condemn that person, but instead, pray for them.

> *"Bless them that curse you, and pray for them which despitefully use you." [Luke 6:28]*

In other words you just turn the other cheek and go on as if nothing was done.

FORGIVE THE DEBT

You may be bitter at someone whom you have co-signed a note for. They've not paid the bill, and you have to pay it. Forgive them of that debt and go on with your life. When you signed the note, you knew that you would be responsible if that person did not pay. I am sure that you felt they would pay, or you would not have guaranteed the loan. If this has happened to you, I am sure that you will never let it happen again. It is very painful to have to experience this; but you must release that person. If you don't strife is inevitable, God cannot bless you, and you will have lost the blessings, because you have shut down your own faith.

The Bible tells you not to guarantee someone else's loan. However, if you have, I'm sure that you did not know what the Bible said about it.

"Be sure you know a person well before you vouch for his credit! Better refuse than suffer later." [Proverbs 11:15, The Living Bible]

Even if you know a person, it is still not advisable. Why? If you do, and they don't pay, you are the one who will suffer later.

"Unless you have the extra cash on hand, don't countersign a note. v. 27, Why risk everything you own? They'll even take your bed." [Proverbs 22: 26 & 27, The Living Bible]

PARDON

For the believer to reach spiritual maturity, he has no choice but to forgive those who have wronged him.

"Judge not, and ye shall not be judged: condemn not, and ye shall not be condemned: forgive, and ye shall be forgiven:" [Luke 6:37]

Jesus said to forgive, and you would be forgiven. The word **forgive** here was translated from the Greek work [Apoluo] which means to relieve, release, dismiss, let die, pardon, depart, divorce, let go, put away, set at liberty. As you can see from these words; when you forgive, you will forget. It will be as if nothing ever happened. One meaning that has particular significance to me is pardon. When a person who committed a crime has been granted a pardon, he is restored or has been given his rights back. It is as though it never happened. A person who commits a crime and spends time in the penitentiary pays for his crime even after he has served his sentence, because it is still on his record. There are several crimes which a person can commit and after doing so, will not be able to vote or work on a government job. By law then, he is never really free.

When you forgive someone, you pardon them. You let it die; it is put away or remembered no more.

"And forgive us our debts, as we forgive our debtors." [Matthew 6:12]

This word **forgive** comes from the Greek word [Aphiemi] which means to lay aside, leave, put away, remit, yield up. Once again there is no holding on once you have forgiven a person. No matter who he is, or what he has done, forgiveness puts the sin away forever.

In Acts 7, Stephen had been stoned and was dying. His last words were, "Lay not this sin to their charge." He totally forgave those who were taking his life. When you look at examples of forgiveness in the scriptures and compare them to today's situations, you see how people let little things divide them. Stephen asked the Lord not to put this on his murderers' account. Be like Stephen and set people free. By doing so you will be set free!

In Genesis 37, Joseph was sold to the Ishmeelites by his brothers, because they did not understand him. He was called to be a leader, and they were jealous of him. As a young man, he was forced to be separated from his father whom he loved very much, he was even put into prison. Yet when he became a grown man and a Governor of Egypt with the power to destroy them, his brothers came to him for help, and he gave them food and forgave them.

I trust you will search your heart and if there is anything there against anyone, you will forgive them. Let's walk together as one, united with all walls broken down and free from the past!

Chapter 7

WALKING IN LOVE

Love is so much more than the expression of words. It is that plus deeds and actions. It is easy to tell someone that you love them; even with deeds and actions when they return that love. But some people have never come to the place of maturity where they love the "unlovely". Jesus loved the unlovely because He controlled His emotions. He knew that love dwelled inside Him and chose to let love rule rather than His flesh. You can never trust your emotions; they will change from minute to minute. However, you can trust the love of God within you that **never** changes!

"For I am the Lord, I change not;...." [Malachi 3:6]

When people do or say things that you do not approve of, or say things that tend to ridicule, it can be dealt with from the emotional level or with the love of God. If you deal with it on an emotional level, you will never rise above the circumstances. If you deal with it through God's love, the whole situation will look different, you will rise above the emotional level, and you will come out a winner.

The problem that most people face after being born again is not learning to take control of their emotions. Instead of seeing any wrong done to them as an attack from Satan, they see it as coming directly from the person and retaliate or strike back at the person. By reacting in this manner they only show that they are on the same level of the person who has offended them. It is a no-win situation. God's love that abides in you can look beyond what is said and done to you; human love cannot.

I read a story about Smith Wigglesworth's wife. It began by Smith telling her that she was not allowed to go to church. He said that if she did, he would lock her out of the house. She felt that she should go to church anyway, so she did. When she returned, the house was locked as he had warned her. She could neither get in the house, nor would he get up and open the door for her. She stayed outside all night.

When he got up the next morning, he opened the door for her. She went in the house cold and tired but did not speak of the inconvenience that he had caused her. Instead she lovingly asked him, "Smith, what would you like for breakfast?" It was by her attitude and resultant actions that he was moved, convicted, and came to God. He became a great Apostle of Faith, because his wife walked in love.

The power of love has not been made available to the person who has not been born again. When this person is faced with an unpleasant situation, he does not have the love of God within to contend with it. It is only natural then that he operates from a selfish viewpoint, protecting himself. There is no source to draw from.

I see many Christians who never mature in the love walk, and it is tragic. They never reach into their spirits and use the power of love that resides there. Instead they continue to respond in a selfish way. Many of the hurts that I experienced in my early walk with God could have been avoided if I had only known more about this particular subject. When I was criticized or spoken evil of, I took it personally and would fight back which was no different from the way I reacted in my former environment. As a result, it caused a lot of hurt, pain, and frustration for me and everyone else involved. My growth was hindered because of my attitude.

I was so happy when revelation began to come to me about God's love and the power that I had within me. I learned that I had control over my life and did not have to be affected by what was said or done to me. I could ignore it as if nothing ever happened. Won't it be pleasing to the Father when everyone comes to this place of growth? It is then that the body of Christ will see true unity and be in one accord!

WHERE ARE YOU IN THE LOVE WALK?

Ask yourself now, "Am I selfish? Am I controlled by my emotions? Am I always allowing my feelings to be affected? Do I cry every time something is said about me?" According to the Word of God these types of reactions are childish, and Paul said to put away childish things. Mature...grow up in love...you **can** change. It will not happen overnight, but you will change if you will deal with the problem that faces you now. Don't try to justify your actions or deeds. Look at it as Jesus would; do what Jesus would do. Don't put it off. Right now let Christ be revealed in you. Overcome evil with good.

> *"Be not overcome of evil, but overcome evil with good." [Romans 12:21]*

Don't look at other people to see how they respond to negative situations. If they have allowed their feelings to control them and you do as they did, you have followed after them. This is not right. Look at God's Word and follow His instructions. He will give you the strength and courage to deal with any circumstance. God would never ask you to do something you couldn't do.

LOVE IS DEMONSTRATED

> *"Though I speak with the tongues of men and of angels, and have not charity, I am become as sounding brass, or a tinking cymbal." [I Corinthians 13:1]* The person who has a silver tongue, who always seems to say the right things to people is not able to demonstrate love by his words only. A person who uses the words, "I love you" often may prophesy, preach, sing in the choir, have a special ministry, or be a lay person with no special call upon his life; but these alone are not verifications of love. It is good that you use

those words often **if** you mean them, but you must have the actions to back them up. When someone has a need, you must love them by doing what needs to be done, not just by making the verbal expression, "I love you, brother" to them. Paul said that if you don't do what is right, your confession is only a religious noise. The church has been religious too long. It is now time to let love be at work in it.

> *"And this is his commandment, that we should believe on the name of his Son Jesus Christ, and love one another, as he gave us commandment." [I John 3:23]*

Again we are told to love one another. It is a commandment, and it is attainable. God will not tell you to do something that He has not given you the ability to accomplish. He has given you the ability to love anybody and everybody at all times and in all situations. The more that you act on this commandment, the stronger you become in all areas of your life! *Make the choice to love!*

I've heard people say, "I just can't love so-and-so." They can't because they choose not to. Separate that person from his sin, and you will see him as God does. This is not to say that you should condone any wrong he might have done...but you can love him.

> *"You are of God, little children, and have over-come them: because greater is he that is in you, than he that is in the world." [I John 4:4]*

You are of God; He lives in you. Greater is He that is **within** you than he that is in the world. It is in Him that we live, and move, and have our being. In Him we can do all things. You, as believers, don't have to rely on your own power. It is not by your might, but it is by His love, His spirit, and His power in you that you overcome.

When you see a brother fall, God's love in you will go and pick him up. Instead of criticizing him and his faults or mistakes, the believer will consider himself and think that if he had fallen, he would desire someone to love him. You will go with a spirit of meekness and restore him. You will not be concerned about your reputation but will think about your brother.

> *"Brethren, if a man be overtaken in a fault, ye which are spiritual, restore such an one in the spirit of meekness; considering thyself, lest thou also be tempted." [Galatians 6:1]*

HELP THOSE IN NEED

How many times has a brother or sister had a need, and you were aware of the situation but pushed it aside and said, "Oh well, someone else will help them, I am too busy!" Love makes a special effort or goes out of the way to help those in need.

> *"But whoso hath this world's goods, and seeth his brother have need, and shutteth up his bowels of compassion from him, how dwelleth the love of God in him?*
>
> *18, My little children, let us not love in word, neither in tongue; but in deed and truth." [I John 3:17 & 18]*

God's love may be demonstrated by a visit to the

hospital to see a friend or loved one, spending time with someone in jail, or showing kindness to someone who has lost a loved one. The fact that you cared about them could change their entire life. Remember, it's not saying, "I love you" only; it is doing what you are able to do to help those who you know are in need.

In John 4, Jesus ministered to the woman at the well. He had to travel 27 miles out of his way, but He did it so that she might find truth. He gave her a drink of water. She would not thirst again; it was an act of love for Jesus to travel that distance; it was a great sacrifice.

In Luke 10, Jesus told of a Jewis man traveling from Jerusalem to Jericho. The man was beaten, robbed, and left for dead. A priest passed by and saw the man but would not help him. A Levite also passed by and looked at the man but left him to die. However, there was a Samaritan on a journey who passed by the man. When he saw the Jew who was left to die, he had compassion on him and forgot about his own busy schedule. He bathed his wounds, put him on his beast, took him to a hospital and paid the bill. He told the workers at the hospital that if the amount of money he was giving them wouldn't cover the bill, he would pay the rest when he returned to that area. This stranger took time with a man in need.

Many people in the body of Christ today have been so occupied with their own needs that they don't want to get involved with others. They live their lives at such a fast pace and with so many obligations, they can't take time to get involved with other needs. This is not obeying the commandment of love. Ask yourself now if you are walking in love. Don't shut your bowels of compassion, but take time to care for those around you.

DON'T HOLD OTHERS IN DEBT TO YOU

Although I am not proud to tell you this story; I will because I believe that it will help you. A number of years ago when I was traveling in large tents and auditoriums, my younger brother went to work for me when he graduated from high school. After working with me for a while, he was drafted into the service. While in the military service, he needed some financial help with which I was able to give him. After being discharged from the service, he came back to work for me as my tent manager. On the whole he did an excellent job. If he made a mistake, though, I would say to him, "After all I have done for you, how could you do this?" I really didn't realize what I was saying to him, nor did I realize that I was keeping him in debt to me.

We were having a crusade in Washington, D.C., and I had come back to the tent after the night meeting, (which I often did). I felt very strange, like someone was going to try to steal some of our equipment. I went to my brother and told him, "Make sure you and one of your men watch things tonight." He said, "I will, go on to your room and rest." He stayed up for a while but did not get one of his men to patrol the area, because he decided to do it himself. In the meantime, he went outside the tent to sit in one of the travel trailers just for a few minutes. He had no intention of doing so, but he fell asleep. While he was asleep, someone came and took all of our musical equipment, part of our public address system, and other valuable items. Several thousands of dollars-worth of equipment was taken, and we did not have any insurance.

When I came into the morning meeting, he met me and said, "I have some bad news for you. I accidentally fell asleep last night, and someone stole some equipment. When I woke up, it was gone." I said to him, "Norman, how could you let this happen after all I have done for you?" He said, "Wait a minute, Don, I have heard what you have done for me until I am tired of it. I am guilty for not doing my job, and I will pay for it. You should be upset with me for neglecting my responsibility. If I am going to have to pay for what you did for me while I was in the service for the rest of my life, though, I wish you'd never helped me!"

Boy, did that hit hard! I was stunned, as I did not realize what I had been doing. I grabbed him, threw my arms around him, and repented of what I had been doing. We were very close, but I had been driving a wedge between us. What I did for him was done out of love, but I was unknowingly using it to keep him in debt to me. He forgave me, and never again did I mention to him what I had done for him. The only time that it has been thought of or spoken about is to tell others how they may be making the same mistake. Whether it is known or unknown, it needs to be dealt with.

How many times have parents been good to their children and kept them in debt. Love them unconditionally, train them properly, show them the right way, but give them the right to make their own decisions when they are able to do so. As a child begins to develop, he must be given room to continue his growth. It is sometimes difficult for parents to back off and loosen the reins; but love will give them room. When the time comes that they fall in love and are ready for marriage, love will allow them to go and live their own life.

If, during this process of growth, children turn away from the things of God, don't confuse them with their sin. You must separate the two. You don't have to approve of or condone their wrong; but they must be assured of your love. **LOVE WILL WIN THEM BACK!** Nagging and complaining will only drive them further away.

"Train up a child in the way he should go: and when he is old, he will not depart from it." [Proverbs 22:6]

If you have lived the life of God in front of your children and taught them the correct way, you can hold on to this promise as they grow.

Whatever they do; whether it is dating someone who is not of the faith, or hanging around the wrong crowd, you can talk with them and remind them with love how the scripture tells them not to be yoked together with unbelievers. [II Corinthians 6:14] Let me emphasize, **you must love, not nag.** If they get involved in drugs and alcohol, don't give up, but don't condone the sin either. They are still your children; don't disown them. Love them, and you will win. Remember that you have God's love; His love does not wear down.

LOVE NEVER FAILS OR FADES OUT

"Love endures long and is patient and kind; love never is envious nor boils over with jealousy; is not boastful or vainglorious, does not display itself haughtily.

5, It is not conceited—arrogant and inflated with pride; it is not rude, (unmannerly), and does not act unbecomingly. Love [God's love in us] does not insist on its own rights or its own way, for it is not self-seeking; it is not touchy or fretful or resentful; it takes no account of the evil done it—pays no attention to a suffered wrong.

6, It does not rejoice at injustice and unrighteousness, but rejoices when right and truth prevail.

7, Love bears up under anything and everything that comes, is ever ready to believe the best of every person, its hopes are fadeless under all circumstances and it endures everything [without weakening].

8, Love never fails—never fades out or becomes obsolete or comes to an end..." [I Corinthians 13:4-8, Amplified]

From verse 4, you can see that there is no room for competition in the body of Christ, because God wants **all** of His children to prosper. Everyone should be working towards the same goals of winning the lost to Jesus and bringing unity to the body. The Bible says that promotion comes from God. He will promote you, and you will not have to compete with anyone! It is so easy to become negligent and let your feelings control you. But when you let love work in your life, you will not be touchy or moody. I have been around a lot of Christians that you never do know what to say to because they are so touchy and moody.

In one of my recent camp meetings, one of the speakers, Jim Munsey, was ministering on love. He said, "If several people were standing and having a conversation together; and one person invited only part of the group out for fellowship at a restaurant or his home, those who were not invited should not be offended but go on their way as if nothing ever happened." You should always consider the feelings of others in a situation such as this. This is only an illustration, however. If for some reason someone wanted to fellowship with a lessor group of the ones he was talking with, he should wait until an appropriate time to invite them out for fellowship so that he would not risk hurting others. Have you grown to the place of not being offended yet? If not, begin to ask God to help you in the area of "touchiness."

In the relationship of the husband and wife, God's love must be practiced each day. Your mate may not always be lovely, but God's love will endure; it will be patient with others. God's love, as seen in I Corinthians 13:4-7, will not be puffed up, become arrogant, rude, or insist on its own way. **LOVE GIVES!** I have made this statement many times, and it is true: "The one who gives the most or loves the most is the strongest." It has been taught to both young men and women about their mates: "Don't let them have their way too much, or they will rule you." For one that is carnal, this may be true. However, when you operate in "God's love," you **always** come out the winner! You don't count how many times you give, because God's love bears up under anything and everything. God's love **never** fails or fades out!

Chapter 8

GIVING

Learning to give is another very important step in your spiritual development. Jesus is the example. He is the greatest giver; He gave His life. Giving of yourself, your time, your money should never be done in **bondage,** but out of **love.** God will multiply the gifts that you give back to you. However, this should not be your motive for giving. Your main motive and purpose for giving should be to win the lost and help in the spreading of the gospel.

"How then shall they call on him in whom they have not believed? and how shall they believe in him of whom they have not heard? and how shall they hear without a preacher?

15, And how shall they preach, except they be sent? as it is written, How beautiful are the feet of them that preach the gospel of peace, and bring glad tidings of good things!"

[Romans 10: 14 & 15]

The time you give or the money you sow to help in a ministry makes it possible for someone to be **sent** with the "Good News" of Jesus Christ! Money can build a church, pay for time on radio or television, send missionaries, or help with the salaries of the staff of those who are declaring the gospel of Christ....**YOUR GIFT MAKES ALL THIS POSSIBLE!**

Anyone who is born again should have a desire to give towards the spreading of the gospel. Just think, someone gave and made it possible for you to hear. You should now have that same desire to help the hurting. You may not be able to go yourself, but you **can** give and send someone in **your** place. *"How can they call on him when they have not heard of him? how can they hear without a preacher; and how shall they preach except they be sent?"* *[Romans 10:14 & 15, paraphrased]* I have heard this statement made: "We are not responsible for the past generation; neither are we responsible for the future generation; but we, the Christians of today, **are** responsible for our generation." This statement is so true. It makes a lot of sense that the first priority of a Christian should be to let others know through the spreading of the gospel that Jesus Christ is Lord. When your life has been changed by hearing the uncompromised truth, you should give to send the gospel of Christ around the world so that others may be helped as you were.

God desires to meet **all** of your needs. He wants you to live above and not beneath; to be the head and not the tail. When you are born again, you become a part of **His** royalty, **His** wealth. He made it for you, but there are conditions that must be met in order for you to receive your portion. I would like to say here that when you are saved, you do not have to give up all your material goods. You don't have to get rid of material wealth, but you should not love or trust them more than you trust God. **God is your source...not things.** In the natural realm, when a person loses his job, he has a tendency to think, "What in the world am I going to do now?" or "This is it! The bottom is falling in on me. I'll never get out of this mess." **Don't give place to these thoughts.** They are lies from the devil. Instead, use this as an opportunity for a blessing. Even though you may have lost your job, business, seniority, savings account, etc., remember that **things** are not your source. God is your source no matter what the circumstances. **God and His Word never change.**

Many spiritual leaders have taught that to be a good, humble, mature Christian, you have to be poor. This is another **lie** of Satan. There is no truth in this statement. **God has plenty.** What kind of God would He be to have all the wealth and keep it just for Himself? Some people say that it will be inherited. Well, that's good...but what about now? Now is the time when you have needs, not when you get to heaven. God has made promises for you **here** and **now!**

SHOULD I TITHE?

"Woe unto you, scribes, and Pharisees, hypocrites! for you pay tithe of mint and anise and cummin, and have omitted the weighter matters of the law, judgment, mercy, and faith; these ought ye to have done, and not to leave

93

the other undone." [Matthew 23:23]

Many people feel that tithing is a part of the law, and since they are no longer "under the law", tithing is not necessary. What they seem to look over in the Word is the fact that the principle of tithing was instituted before the law was ever given. An example is Jacob's revelation of God's presence at Bethel in Genesis 28. He said in verse 22, *"....and of all that thou shalt give me I will surely give the tenth unto thee."* Another is Abraham's tithe to Melchizedek in Genesis 14:20. Both of these acts took place many years before the law was given. This would tend to prove by the scriptures that the principle of returning to God a tenth of all that He has blessed man with is as old as the human race. When you give a tenth, you are acknowledging God's blessing upon you and that you want to return a portion for the continual spread of the gospel. You are showing your thanks to Him for what He has done.

Under the law the use of tithe was not a national tax for Israel as some have said. The governing of Israel was accomplished through judges who were raised up as need by the Lord from among many tribes or by kings who came from the tribe of Judah.

"And all the tithe of the land, whether of the seed of the land, or of the fruit of the tree, is the Lord's: it is holy unto the Lord." [Leviticus 27:30]

"And behold, I have given the children of Levi all the tenth in Israel for an inheritance, for their service which they serve, even the service of the tabernacle of the congregation." [Numbers 18:21]

94

When God divided the land among the twelve tribes, He gave the Levites no land to call their own. The tenth of all Israel was to be their pay, because they were God's ministers.

> *"Thus speak unto the Levites, and say unto them, When ye take of the children of Israel the tithes which I have given you from them for your inheritance, then ye shall offer up an heave offering of it for the Lord, even a tenth part of the tithe.*
>
> *27, And this your heave offering shall be reckoned unto you, as though it were the corn of the threshingfloor, and as the fullness of the winepress." [Numbers 18:26 & 27]*

God was saying to the tribe of Levi that Israel was their field; and if they ministered to it faithfully, tended to it well, and encouraged the people to do well, they were deserving of support. If they neglected their duties, though, and Israel fell away from God, they were not deserving. The Levites prospered as did the people, because their income was a percentage of the income of the people.

> *"The tithe is mine. It has always been mine. You pay me by giving my tenth to the Levite who ministers to you." [Numbers 18:26 & 27, paraphrased]* God had more to say in Malachi about tithing and giving of offerings.

> *"Bring ye all the tithes into the storehouse, that there may be meat in mine house, and prove me now herewith, saith the Lord of hosts, if I will not open you the windows of heaven, and pour you out a blessing, that there*

shall not be room enough to receive it."
[Malachi 3:10]

Once again, you are admonished to give tithes and offerings in order for the gospel to be preached. God says
here also that if you will **prove** Him and give **freely**, He
will reward you again for giving back His portion; and
that as you give more, He will open the windows of
heaven and pour out blessings upon you! Again, the
first reason to tithe and give is so that the gospel can
be preached. The added benefit, though, is that when
you give, God **pours** out abundant blessings upon you.

TITHING IN THE NEW TESTAMENT

"And here men that die receive tithes; but
there he receiveth them, of whom it is wit-
nessed that he liveth." [Hebrews 7:8]

In other words, here and now in this present age, God
has **authorized** men who die...Apostles, Prophets,
Evangelists, Pastors, Teachers; His called vessels,
who, like the Levites, are giving their lives to His service, to receive the **tithes.** When a Christian gives his
tithes to one of these ministers whom Jesus has
authorized to receive tithes; acting in His **absence;**
Jesus Himself receives that tithe, and records it in His
account.

WHERE SHOULD I TITHE?

The tithe is the Lord's. As much as all the silver
and gold is God's, your offering is His also. He gives it
to you but leaves it up to you to put it where it will do
the most good for His kingdom. **It should go into God's
work.** Remember that all religious work is not God's

work. God has instructed you to turn away from those who only have a form of God and do not have a true spirit of worship. Those who deny His power should not be included in your support.

"Having a form of godliness, but denying the power thereof: from such turn away." [II Timothy 3:5]

Since you are admonished to turn away from those who are religious or have no depth in the things of God, your offering should never be given to any group that is not doing the same works that Jesus did. It is unscriptural to support so-called religious groups that are fighting, opposing, or ridiculing a servant of God who is doing what Jesus called him to do.

Now that I have shown you where "not" to give your tithes and offerings, you can see that the place to invest your tithes and offerings is where you get fed "spiritually." In other words, the place to give is where you get your "spiritual" training or where you are ministered to. Don't run wild with that statement, though. First of all, you should have a home church where you are getting a steady diet of God's Word. If you are ministered to and fulfilled there, you should then make that the place where you give regularly. That ministry deserves your support with the tithes that belong to God.

You should be committed to a local body with a **Pastor** and be loyal to him. It is there that you are helping to build up the area in which you live. I believe in giving to other ministries also if you are ministered to by them. If you are being fed at your church, though, you should give extra...over and above what you normally give. Don't support another ministry at the expense of your home church. On several occasions I have asked people at my church if they were supporting other ministries. About 50 percent always responded that they did. Almost without fail these are the ones who are greatly blessed. I always encourage my members to support other ministries that bless them. I know that as they give, the windows of heaven open upon them, and God gives them more to give.

I believe in giving to the poor and those who have needs.

"When you help the poor you are lending to the Lord—and he pays wonderful interest on your loan!" [Proverbs 19:17, The Living Bible]

When you give to the poor, you are lending to God, and He will give you back much more than you have sown. This should not be loaned or given as tithes from your income but as an expression of love. Remember, **your tithes are for the spreading of the gospel.**

I have had people come and tell me, "Well, I'd like to support you. I come here regularly, and you really do feed me, but I put my tithes and offerings where the greatest need is. Besides, you have more people to support you than so-and-so does, so I've been giving there." If you give because of a need and not because you're being fed, it is **unscriptural**, and you will not reap the benefit. It is alright to give when there is a need, but that should not be the only reason to give. Neither should a person have to always be made aware of a need before they give. I encourage **giving** to a need that will help hurting people but be sensitive to God and give out of obedience. In this way, you will find joy in your giving. I repeat, don't **rob** your church and the ministry where you are being fed to give to another need.

WHAT IS YOUR MOTIVE FOR GIVING?

"Let each one [give] as he has made up his own mind and purposed in heart, not reluctantly or sorrowfully or under compulsion, for God loves, (that is, He takes pleasure in, prizes above other things, and is unwilling to abandon or do without) a cheerful, (joyous, prompt-to-do-it) giver—whose heart is in his giving."
[II Corinthians 9:7, Amplified]

In this scripture Paul tells you to be aware of the motive in which you give. He said to purpose in your mind what you are going to give and why. Don't be reluctant to give when God is speaking to you, but rather, be obedient. He also says not to give because you feel sorry for someone, because there is a need, or because of someone putting pressure on you. If you do, you may regret it later...and if you regret it later, you may not reap. It is the **cheerful, hilarious** and **excited** giver that God loves. It pleases Him when a person gives from his heart with no strings attached.

Giving of your tithes and offerings does not give you a right to control those you are supporting. If it is a gift from your heart, it is to aid in the work of God and is no longer yours. The amount of your gift is not always what is important; it is the attitude in which you give. A person could give an offering of $1,000.00, but the person who gave only $10.00 may have made the biggest sacrifice. If you gave $1,000.00 to give a voice, then the one who gave $10.00 should get the voice. One should not expect the right to do so anyway. God has given the one in authority the vision for that ministry, and the gifts should be to make that goal possible. It is a tragic mistake that has been made by many good and honest people. They think that because they tithe to their local church, they should have a vote in how it is spent. **No!** They are not your tithes—they are God's. When you give it, you are giving back to God and those whom you trust should have enough spiritual integrity to do with the money what God has told them to do. You should give there, because you are being fed there; not to have a voice in leadership; your motive is wrong if that is why you are giving.

A person told me that he would purchase a piece of property for the church if I would change the name of it to one that he picked out. I could not do that. If God was telling him to give it, then the name of the church would not have mattered. When you give into the kingdom of God, don't complain about it or throw it up to the one who you are giving it to. **Give freely** into the kingdom of God. Turn your gift loose just as a farmer plants seed into the ground. He doesn't take it back or dig it up or complain about it. He leaves it there and waits until the seeds come up. He turns it loose to the ground.

HOW MUCH SHOULD I TITHE?

I believe that in tithing you should not only tithe on what you have made, but rather tithe on what you

100

are believing to receive. You **must** use good judgment in doing this, though. If you are presently at one level, and you desire to raise your income level ten times, you should start your increase on the level you **can.** If you put it too high to begin with, you can hinder your faith. Remember, I told you to walk in your level of faith so that whatever you can conceive and believe for, you can have!

If a person expects an increase on his tithing, he should be **consistent.** I also believe that Christians should tithe on their gross income instead of their net. I believe there are businesses today, owned by **believers,** that are not prospering because the owner does not tithe from his/her business. They take a salary or money out of the business, and tithe on that. This is good; and you should. But if the business is not making a profit, start tithing out of it. Do something to give it the opportunity to prosper. I have had people to tell me, "Well, I have not shown a profit, so how can I prosper?" What about the equity you have built up, or the equipment you have purchased in your business? Both have value.

> *"Give, and it shall be given unto you; good measure, pressed down, and shaken together, and running over, shall men give into your bosom. For with the same measure that ye mete withal it shall be measured to you again." [Luke 6:38]*

Some people have said, "We started tithing, and God really did bless us; but all at once, something went wrong. Our car broke down, and we had to have a new motor put in it. That cost us several hundred dollars.

101

Then our washing machine went out, and we had to get a new one. And our heater went out. And we were tithing!'' These are all attacks from Satan. He does not want you to give, so he will do anything to stop you...**if he can.** When attacks come, keep right on giving. If Satan can stop you in the early stages while you are young in this area, he will, because it will be harder for him to stop you when your faith grows to a higher level. Before you can get up, Satan tries to knock you down. Don't be discouraged, though. Instead, **get up, keep giving,** and God will give you extra income. Do you remember what I said at the beginning of the book? When you were learning to walk and you fell, you did not quit trying. No! You got up and tried again and again until you learned to walk.

Sometimes there are other reasons why people have financial problems, even when they are tithers and givers. They may be bad managers of money, or they are not good managers of their business affairs. They may be excellent in the services they perform but have little knowledge of the business and handling money. A person could be the best surgeon there is; but if he doesn't have business knowledge, he will be hindered financially. However, if you will go to God about your problem, He will show you what it is and how to change it.

DON'T GIVE OUT OF OBLIGATION

When you go to a meeting, an offering is being received, and there is a special appeal made to build a building or pay for a special program, purpose in your heart what you can do. If you do not have the amount that you would like to give and your faith level is not there to believe for it, don't do anything that would cause you to struggle. I am not saying that you shouldn't give sacrificially. Do what God tells you to do, though, not what you think you "have" to. There are many times that people make pledges to a ministry and mean well, but they do not pay the pledge because it was an emotional response rather than one from the heart.

There are those ministries whom God speaks to you to become partners with or make a commitment to, but some who respond later change their mind and are not obedient to God. They will have some excuse why they are not fulfilling their promise.

"When you vow a vow or make a pledge to God, do not put off paying it; for God has no pleasure in fools [those who witlessly mock Him]. Pay what you vow.

5, It is better that you should not vow than that you should vow and not pay.

6, Do not allow your mouth to cause your body to sin, and do not say before the messenger [the priest] that it was an error or mistake. Why should God be [made] angry at your voice and destroy the work of your hands?" [Ecclesiastes 5:4-6, Amplified]

It is better not to make a commitment than to back down after you have made it. Don't allow your mouth to cause you to sin. Don't make a commitment unless you mean it. Remember, giving should not be a burden or strain; it should be a **joy**. Once again, I will say I am not telling you that you shouldn't give sacrificially. What I am saying is **don't** put yourself into bondage.

Pray **before** you make the commitment. Know where your faith is; and if you don't have it, don't do something because others are. If God tells you to make a pledge, or your faith level is there to make one, even if you don't have it, you will get it as God will provide for you.

> *"And [God] Who provides seed for the sower and bread for eating will also provide and multiply your [resources for] sowing, and increase the fruits of your righteousness [which manifests itself in active goodness, kindness and charity].*
>
> *11, Thus you will be enriched in all things and in every way, so that you can be generous, [and your generosity as it is] administered by us will bring forth thanksgiving to God.*
>
> *12, For the service the ministering of this fund renders does not only fully supply what is lacking to the saints (God's people), but it also overflows in many [cries of] thanksgiving to God. [II Corinthians 9:10-12, Amplified]*

These verses of scripture tell you that God will provide seed for the sower; and He will enrich you in all things and in every way so you can be a generous giver.

God tells you to give sacrificially, and when you do, He will multiply your resources. Giving is a joy. You must give because you want to, not because you have to. Oral Roberts made an unparalleled statement when he said, "It's not a debt you owe; it's a seed you sow." So don't put yourself in debt by speaking or making a commitment before you think. Always remember to

give only out of love. **You can give without loving, but
*you can't love without giving.***

GOD FAVORS A GENEROUS GIVER

> *"[Remember] this: he who sows sparingly and
> grudgingly will also reap sparingly and grudg-
> ingly, and he who sows generously and that
> blessings may come to someone, will also reap
> generously and with blessings." [II Corin-
> thians 9:6, Amplified]*

Paul is saying here not to be stingy with the substance
that you have. Sow generously in order for blessings to
come to others, and you too! If you sow sparingly and
grudgingly, you will not enjoy God's blessing and favor
upon you. Don't hold too tight to what you have—learn
the principle of **giving.**

> *"It is possible to give away and become richer!
> It it also possible to hold on too tightly and
> lose everything.*
>
> *25, Yes, the liberal man shall become rich! By
> watering others, he waters himself." [Proverbs
> 11:24 & 25, The Living Bible]*

In 1963, Sharon and I were travelling on the
evangelistic field. We were on our way to put up our
small tent for a Revival Crusade and stopped at a tent
meeting where a friend of mine was speaking. While
talking with us, he told us that he wanted to get a new
tent. I looked around his tent, and it seemed to be in
perfect shape. I wondered why he would want another
one. Of course, I was comparing it with our tent. It was
small and would seat about 150 people. There were so

many holes in it that when it rained, people felt as if they were sitting outside instead of inside. I looked at the difference in size and condition of his tent to mine. I said to myself, "It sure would be nice to have a tent like this to work for God. I would be happy with one like this." He asked the congregation for an offering for his new tent. As he did, I felt impressed to give $100.00. I had barely $100.00 to get to our destination and put my little tent up. I did not hesitate, though, and ran quickly to the front of the tent with many others. He received enough money to purchase the new tent. He then said, "Don, since you obeyed God, He is telling me to give you this tent." Boy, did I get excited! I did not sow into his ministry because of a need that he had, but because God impressed upon me to. It did not matter to me that he had more than I did; I gave the money because I wanted to.

As we were leaving the service that night, we did not tell anyone that we had several hundred miles left to travel and only had a few dollars. However, all at once, people began to give us money. We received several hundred dollars as well as a new tent that would seat nearly 800 people. The minister also took his big truck and brought the tent to us. We gave generously, and God rewarded us with favor because of our obedience.

> "*And God is able to make all grace (every favor and earthly blessing) come to you in abundance, so that you may always and under all circumstances and whatever the need, be self-sufficient—possessing enough to require no aid or support and furnished in abundance*

for every good work and charitable donation."
[II Corinthians 9:8, Amplified]

I am not saying that any time before you give, you must hear God tell you to. That is inconsistent with what the Word tells you. I do believe, though, that you should not let an offering pass by without giving at least something. When God tells you to give sacrificially, He will give you favor with men and cause blessing to come to you in **abundance** so that you may always and under all circumstances, whatever the need, be self-sufficient.

"Give, and [gifts] will be given you, good measure, pressed down, shaken together and running over will they pour into [the pouch formed by] the bosom [of your robe and used as a bag]. For with the measure you deal out—that is, with the measure you use when you confer benefits on others—it will be measured back to you." [Luke 6:38, Amplified]

Jesus said that when you give, He will cause men to give unto your bosom. When you measure out your gifts, they will come back in good measure, pressed down, and shaken together. It could be that someone will give you money; or you could have favor with someone who will give you a job; a promotion on a job; or a business opportunity. Remember that Jesus is saying this: *"After you give...expect it to come back to you!"* This is a spiritual law. Whatever you sow, you will reap.

GOD'S WILL FOR YOU TO PROSPER

"Beloved, I wish above all things that thou mayest prosper and be in good health, even as thy soul prospereth." [III John 2]

John said that he wished above all things that you would prosper. Prospering is more than having material things. Its complete meaning is having the power and ability to meet every need: **spiritually, physically, emotionally, financially, and socially.** John said that your prosperity would come as your soul prospers. If you seek and desire the material things of this world, you have selfish desires. This is wrong thinking,and it will hinder Godly blessings. If your mind has not been renewed to the things of God, lust and greed will take over with unhappy results.

"For the love of money is the root of all evil: which while some coveted after, they have erred from the faith, and pierced themselves through with many sorrows." [I Timothy 6:10]

Don't seek wealth—but rather seek "the kingdom of God." When you seek God's kingdom, He will give you other things.

"But seek for (aim at and strive after) first of all His kingdom, and His righteousness [His way of doing and being right], and then all these things taken together will be given you besides." [Matthew 6:33, Amplified]

God desires that you put Him first in all things. When you do, He will give you the things that you desire. This does not necessarily mean that someone will just "give" you everything. That is entirely possible, but

He will more than likely give you wisdom, knowledge, friends, etc., which can cause you to obtain that prosperity for your life.

"But my God shall supply all your needs according to His riches in glory by Christ Jesus." [Philippians 4:19]

God will supply your needs by Jesus Christ. When you learn the principle of giving and seek to please God, you will be given an opportunity by the Lord for great things. This is probably because your mind is the mind of Christ, and things will not cause you to be puffed up. The more you have, the more humble you become. "Things" will not change you; the Word will do that. This does not mean that you should sit idly and wait for things to come to you. Don't take the attitude that if God wants you to have it, He will give it to you. No! Go...and God will go with you. He will open doors that may have been closed to you. He will guide your steps to the blessings that He has for you.

HEAR GOD'S VOICE

Remember this: **God will always give you opportunities to sow.** In 1970, I was speaking in Buffalo, New York, in the Memorial Auditorium. I was staying with my in-laws just across the border in Canada. I travelled this route each day to the meetings. After the morning meeting, I was on my way back home when a voice inside me spoke up and said, "Go the New York thru way." Normally I took the route that would take me across the Peace Bridge into Canada, because it was a shorter distance. I didn't pay much attention to the voice. Again and again, though, it said, "Go the New York thru way." Finally I said, "Alright, I will go the thru way."

Just as I turned off to go the thru way I saw that there was construction work going on. I had to slow my car down almost to a stop. On my left I noticed a young couple, and before I realized what I was doing, I put my window down and asked them if they would like a ride. They accepted. There was little conversation as I drove down the highway. As time passed I heard the voice of God again, and He told me to give them some money. At first I didn't want to, because I did not know the people. I knew that God had spoken to me, though, and as we got to the place where they were to get out, I reached into my pocket and gave them all of the cash that I had with me. When I did, I told them that the Lord told me to give it to them. They looked surprised, and the man said to his wife, "This is real money!" I said, "Yes, it is."

I found out that they had hitch-hiked from Florida. Their house had burned there, and they lost everything they owned. With no insurance they saw no reason to stay there and were returning to the area where they were originally from. They told me that several hours before I came along, they had run out of money and had nothing to eat. They took hands and prayed, saying that if there was a God like the one they had learned about in Sunday School, He would send help to them now. A little while later they went to a house and asked for food. The person at the house ran them off. This discouraged them, and they had given up all hope that there was a God. They decided that it was no use to pray and didn't know what else to do. All at once, here they were being picked up by a total stranger. Then when they were getting out of his car, he gives them money, and tells them that God told him to give it to them. As a result, on the New York thru way, they cried out and accepted Jesus into their lives. Obedience caused two people to accept Jesus as Savior. I was rewarded on the spot for seeds that I sowed.

POVERTY IS NOT A VIRTUE

It has been taught by many that you must be poor if you are a Christian. The truth is that being poor does not make you a better Christian; having your needs met makes you a better one. God has plenty; He's my Father; I'm His son. I [just as you are] am an heir of God and joint heir [co-heir] with Jesus. This means that what God has is available to you **if** you meet the conditions. If you don't meet the conditions, you will not have the blessings of God upon your life.

"If ye be willing and obedient, ye shall eat the good of the land." [Isaiah 1:19]

Being poor is not a virtue. It will not keep you humble. It instead hurts your self-image and your marriage. You are not able to get the vehicle or clothes that you need, and you can't pay your bills on time. Most of the time you are not able to give to God. You get no pleasure out of this. God gets no pleasure when His children are doing without either. He wants the best for His children.

"Let them shout for joy, and be glad, that

> *favour my righteous cause: yea, let them say*
> *continually, Let the Lord be magnified, which*
> *hath pleasure in the prosperity of his servant."*
> *[Psalms 35:27]*

When an earthly father sees his children do well, he is happy and rejoices with them. God is the same, and He has more than enough. He wants us to have it also. Don't let Satan deceive and rob you of God's blessing by telling you that it is not God's will for you to prosper. I have already covered the fact that if money and material things are first place in your life, then you have erred and are not in the right relationship with God. The big lie that Satan has told Christians is that it is wrong for them to prosper.

THE POVERTY OF THE POOR IS THEIR RUIN

Poverty ruins the believer because he is down. He can never do the things that he desires. Also one who believes that poverty is the will of God has nothing to invest in God's work. Poverty has kept the gospel from being preached the way in which it needs to be. It is a part of the curse of the law, and you have been redeemed from the curse of the law through Jesus Christ. He took your poverty at Calvary and became poor that you might have plenty.

> *"For you are becoming progressively to be ac-*
> *quainted with and to recognize more strongly*
> *and clearly the grace of our Lord Jesus*
> *Christ—His kindness, His gracious generosi-*
> *ty, His undeserved favor and spiritual bless-*

ing; [in] that though He was [so very] rich, yet for your sakes He became [so very] poor, in order that by His poverty you might become enriched—abundantly supplied." [II Corinthians 8:9, Amplified]

God is good, kind, and generous. He became poor so that you could have an abundant supply of what is needed. I urge you to stand up for your rights as a believer. Don't let circumstances or Satan's lies keep you from your inheritance. Be a cheerful giver to God's work, help those who are in need, be partners in the ministry, and God will rebuke the devourer from you.

DOES GOD RETURN ONE HUNDRED FOLD?

"And other fell on good ground, and did yield fruit that sprang up and increased; and brought forth, some thirty, and some sixty, and some an hundred." [Mark 4:8]

Yes, there is a hundred fold return. As you examine this scripture, though, Jesus said that when the Word is sown into good ground, it produces some thirty, some sixty, and some a hundred. Now, if there is a thirty fold, then there is a ten, twenty, forty, fifty, seventy, eighty, and ninety fold. The extent that you receive is up to you, the believer.

Now stay with me; I am not going to get negative. Rather, I am going to show you how to get a higher return on what you sow into the kingdom. First of all, your returns will not always come in money and material things; there are other ways that God gives back to you. To release your return when you give, you must be able to see the return. I'm sure that you have heard the statement, "If I could see it, I would believe it." There is some truth to it. This does not mean that you have to have the literal returns in your hand before you will believe it. You must, though, be able to see it through the eyes of faith.

Let me ask you this: "Have you ever been able to conceive or see a hundred fold on everything you gave?" More than likely your answer is, "No." I know that this may sting; but the truth is that if you don't "see" it, you will never "believe" it, and you won't "obtain" it. Why not start out with something that you **can** believe for by faith...even if it's only ten fold. Once you have succeeded in that capacity, keep raising your sights. When you get close to your ten fold, move it up and keep moving it up until you have reached your full potential. Remember, you must have a starting place. I would rather have a ten fold return than nothing at all. You can't start at the finish line. Success comes after starting and running in the race.

Some think that giving is a get-rich-quick scheme which happens overnight. There are supernatural miracles that happen all of the time, however, you receive according to your faith. Where is your faith level? Don't try to walk by someone else's faith; you must walk on your own. God is no respector of persons and He will do no less for you the same than He has done for anyone. Your part is to see it, believe it, and not to be moved by the circumstances.

Some have made the tragic mistake of believing that if they gave all their possessions, they would get rich overnight. I'm sure that they had good intentions; but one must really be led of God when making a decision such as that. God looks at the heart. I have seen some people who have given the majority of their possession; but because they did not have overnight success, they complained and kept their blessings away. **Please don't complain after you give.** Give your seed time to grow to maturity.

> *"And Jesus answered and said, verily I say unto you, There is no man that hath left house, or brethren, or sisters, or father, or mother, or wife, or children, or lands, for my sake, and the gospel's,*
>
> *30, But he shall receive an hundredfold now in this time, houses, and brethren, and sisters, and mothers, and children, and lands, with persecutions; and in the world to come eternal life." [Mark 10:29 & 30]*

Jesus said that you could receive the hundred fold in this life. He explains in this scripture that it would not just be in material things; but you would have brothers, sisters, mothers, fathers, houses, and lands. I have many **spiritual** mothers, fathers, sisters, and brothers. I have friends who own cottages and condominiums in different resorts and will let me stay there any time I want to. Actually, I would rather it be that way for me. Sharon and I have returns which come in many different ways, and we are grateful for all of the benefits.

DON'T BE SATISFIED
WITH MEDIOCRACY

Many people are satisfied with a car that runs, a roof over their heads, wearable clothes, and being able to give $40.00 to $50.00 a week to God. Don't be satisfied with being at or below the average. Get out of that rut, out of your "comfort zone". Take a giant step in faith and open that business, go after that promotion, work towards that raise, or buy that company so you can give more to God. Maybe you have never thought about owning your own business, or rising above your present level of life. Trust God and ask Him for a dream. He will give you one and show you how it can be fulfilled to not only prosper you, but also to further the spread of the gospel. Take charge of your life through the promises of God in His Word, and He will join with you to take the kingdom by force. [Matthew 11:12]

Chapter 9

PATIENCE

Many Christians, both those young in the Lord and those more experienced in their walk with God, listen to tapes, read books, go to meetings, and hear testimonies of what God has done for others. They get excited, and they want to be full grown immediately. They expect all of these things that they are praying and believing for to happen *NOW!* To obtain the things which he desires, the believer must understand *faith* and how it works. Faith is not something that will get you out of a crisis or bring you to overnight success. It is a way of life. It is the trust and confidence in God that He will keep His **WORD** and do what It says. It is gained and developed by putting it into practice. A key factor in using faith to its fullest extent is found in patience.

Patience is having the ability *to stand and wait without complaining,* being steadfast, enduring,

117

perseverant, unmovable from the truth of the Word.
W.E. Vine's Dictionary says that patience is the
quality which does not surrender to **circumstances** or
succumb under trial. I believe that the lack of patience
many times keeps people from receiving God's blessing. Robert Tilton said that there are many packages in
heaven with a big stamp marked "**UNCLAIMED**" on
them, because people gave up before the answers came.
God heard the petitions of faith; but before He could
get the manifestations to them, they gave up.

FAITH IS LIKE A SEED

The farmer is a very good example of patience. He
plants seeds in the spring and waits until the end of
summer or the beginning of fall for the harvest. He
doesn't give up; he simply waits until harvest time.
Have you ever prayed for something and then given up,
because you have not physically seen the answer as of
yet? Well, renew your vision, trust God, and stand
firm. Don't let Satan steal what belongs to you; he can
only take what you let him take. **GOD IS YOUR
SOURCE!**

When you plant corn, you cannot expect it to be
fully grown overnight. Of course not. In a few days,
you see the little blade as it begins to break through the
soil. As you watch it from day to day, you cannot see it
actually growing, but you can tell that it is **growing
and developing** by its increased size. When you plant
the seed, you find that it will take from 80 to 120 days,
before it is ready for harvest. Receiving from God is

really that simple. You **MUST** give God's Word time to grow within in order to produce what you have asked.

Remember, faith is like a seed. *It must be given time to grow.*

"And he said, So is the kingdom of God, as if a man should cast seed into the ground;

27, And should sleep, and rise night and day, and the seed should spring and grow up, he knoweth not how.

28, For the earth bringeth forth fruit of herself; first the blade, then the ear, after that the full corn in the ear." [Mark 4:26-28]

A couple of weeks after you've planted the corn, you go out to look at it and become excited, because you see the blades that have broken through the earth. Even though it is not fully matured, what do you call it? Corn, of course. When you show your planting to someone, you say, "Let me show you my corn." It is not corn yet, but you are already calling it corn; and the plant will produce corn. You are actually "calling those things that be not as though they were." This is what patience will do for you as a believer. Patience will always wait without giving up or becoming discouraged.

DON'T LET "NO" STOP YOUR SUCCESS

The statement, "No," does not always mean that you have no answer to what you have believed for. You may have applied for a job only to find that the company has hired someone else. Don't give up and get discouraged, because someone else was hired. Go back again! That person who was hired may not like the job and quit or be fired. People give up jobs every day through quitting, being fired, transfer, retirement, or death. There is always an opening somewhere. ***BE PATIENT!*** Go fill out another application and tell the prospective employer that you want the job! Be persistent and claim God's favor. Don't be bashful. Go with confidence, and God will go with you.

My younger brother came to a Sunday morning service where he heard me teach on persistence and patience. He had a job at the time but was not satisfied with it. He had filled out applications in different places, and he was called to interview for a job that he really wanted. When he arrived there, he was told that they had just hired someone for that position. However, he did not take that response as the final answer. He told the personnel officer, "I want to leave my resume with you." The response was that there would be no purpose in his doing so.

Trusting in God and not what he was told, he convinced them to let him leave his resume. In spite of the opposition facing him, he left the building praising God. The next day he was called to come in to work! The person whom they had hired quit the job after the first day. My brother's patience and persistence, along with faith in God, obtained the job that he wanted. Be patient and persistent; don't give up. God has exactly what you have ordered!

DON'T BE DISCOURAGED

"Cast not away therefore your confidence, which hath great recompense of reward.

36, For ye have need of patience, that, after ye have done the will of God, ye might receive the promise." [Hebrews 10:35 & 36]

If you lose hope, you lose your confidence and become discouraged. I have watched people lose their hope because of circumstances: maybe a divorce, the loss of a job, or other type of dilemma in their lives. If you are in that place today, don't despair.

"...I will never leave thee, nor forsake thee." [Hebrews 13:5]

This is a promise; believe it and hold on to it. After you have done all you know to do, exercise patience and stand.

Everyone has the opportunity to lose hope and give up. God, though, has given you His grace to win, and to overcome discouragement. Don't let Satan discourage you through circumstances. The word discourage means to deprive of courage, hope, or confidence; dishearten; to advise or persuade a person to refrain; to try to prevent by disapproving or raising objections or obstacles.

When you step out in faith, there are well-meaning people, including Christians, who will advise you not to attempt what you have planned. They will tell you how they tried the same thing or something similar and failed and will raise objections to dishearten you. All of this is the work of Satan to get you to lose your courage

121

and confidence. This is where patience comes in. You **encourage** yourself even though you may not feel like it. Don't wait for someone else to come and encourage you. Take **God's Word** and encourage yourself *NOW!*

I Samuel Chapter 30, tells how David encouraged himself. He was distressed, because the city had been burned. His two wives and children; along with his men, their wives and children had been taken captive. After he prayed, God told him to **PURSUE, OVER-TAKE, and RECOVER ALL.** It was because he encouraged himself that he was able to do it. God gave David the strength, and He will do the same for you. As you encourage yourself, you can hear the voice of God. God will give you direction. If you give in to discouragement, you can't hear God. To encourage means to give courage, hope, or confidence; to give support to.

As David encouraged himself in the Lord, courage, hope, and confidence came to him. He also received the support of his men to go with him to recover their families. As you meditate, confess God's Word, and encourage yourself, new hope and confidence will come to you.

> *"Only be thou strong and very courageous, that thou mayest observe to do according to all the law, which Moses my servant commanded thee: turn not from it to the right hand or to the left, that thou mayest prosper withersoever thou goest.*
>
> *9, Have not I commanded thee? **Be strong and of a good courage;** be not afraid, neither be thou dismayed: for the Lord they God is with thee*

whithersoever thou goest." [Joshua 1:7 & 9]

The word **courage,** as defined from Webster's Dictionary, means the attitude of facing and dealing with anything difficult or painful instead of withdrawing from it; the quality of being fearless, brave, or valiant. I believe God was making a point to Joshua that when you are faced with a difficult situation or when something is painful, don't withdraw from it but be strong and fear not. In other words, encourage yourself in the Lord.

> *"For I am with you wherever you go. Don't look at the circumstances on the right or on the left, but remember my promise that I will prosper you wherever you go." [Joshua 1:9, paraphrased]*

God tells you the same thing; by faith and patience you will inherit His promises.

When Moses sent out the spies in Numbers 13:20, he told them to be of good courage. The word **courage** from the Hebrew word [chazaq] that is translated into English as courage means to conquer, be consistent, continue, fortify, hold fast, be mighty, be stout, be sure, be urgent, withstand. You can again see patience at work here, because, as a Christian, you are to be **constant** in your faith and your confession. As you **continue** your walk with God, you can be **sure** that God means what He says and **withstand** the pressure which Satan brings. You are **stout** with God's power; you are **mighty** in the face of all opposition; the Word of God **fortifies** you and brings you through every situation.

God told Joshua to be **strong** and of good courage. God was telling him that he could stand and be an overcomer every day of his life, and *YOU* can too! Websters Dictionary defines the word strong as tough, firm, able to resist attack, not easily defeated, not weak or dilute, forceful, persuasive, active. The believer who develops his patience will stand **firmly** and **resist** the **attacks** of the enemy. He stays **active and forceful**, showing no signs of **weakness** but presses through with total confidence in God's Word.

Patience is the force that will keep you from veering off to the right or left of what you are believing for. The Word of God is your title deed to the answers; it is all you will ever need. Whatever you are standing in faith for, continue standing. God is faithful to His word; He hastens to perform it. [Jeremiah 1:12] As you hear and do His Word, don't be moved in the midst of your greatest attacks but stand steadfastly, and the power of God will break the yokes.

> *"Stand therefore, hold your ground—having tightened the belt of truth around your loins, and having put on the breastplate of integrity and of moral rectitude and right standing with God;*
>
> *15, And having shod your feet in preparation [to face the enemy with the firm-footed stability, the promptness and the readiness produced by the good news] of the Gospel of peace.*
>
> *16, Lift up over all the (covering) shield of saving faith, upon which you can quench all the flaming missiles of the wicked [one]." [Ephesians 6:14, 15, 16, Amplified]*

Remember that attacks and trials from the enemy do not cause you to have patience. They cause you to use or work the patience that you already have. If you go after something in faith, you must make the decision to **stand** until the answer comes. If you don't make this decision, the attacks will then cause you to lose sight of what you are believing for. Put patience to work, tighten the belt of truth around your loins, be prepared for the enemy, and stand firmly on the Word. Then, as the flaming darts come, your faith and patience withstands them all. You will be more than a conqueror! You can *win*—you are a *winner!* A winner never quits, and a quitter never wins. Don't give up on that unsaved husband, wife, son, daughter, or relative. Don't let Satan cheat you. Take your inheritance! **YOU CAN REIGN IN LIFE!** You are an heir of God and a joint heir with Jesus.

As a Pastor I have had to tighten the belt of truth and walk in patience. Attacks have come, and the situation has looked impossible, but I have always stood, and God's Word has always come through for me. It may not be the time that I want things to happen, but His timing is always perfect.

Several years ago we were buying a building for our church, and we had to have the entire amount of money by a certain date. We had already invested several thousand dollars, and it seemed we had come to the end. We did not have the money to close the deal which meant that we would lose all the we had invested. The day that we were supposed to complete the agreement came. I sat at my desk and said, "Lord, I'm not worried about this situation. You will come through for us; I know You will." I brushed the problem aside and went about my day. It was not very long until the man whom we were buying the property from came in. He said, "I am having a problem with the papers. I can't get a clear deed, and it looks as if it will take me 90 days to complete it."

This was an answer to my prayer, because the extra 90 days gave us the time we needed to raise the extra money. I did not perceive that he would have a problem, but I stood anyway. God moved for me in a mighty way, not by giving me the money on that date, but by giving me more time. At the end of the 90 days, we were ready and closed the deal.

> *"Knowing this, that the trying of your faith worketh patience.*
>
> *4, But let patience have her perfect work, that ye may be perfect and entire, wanting nothing." [James 1:3 & 4]*

My faith **was** tried, but patience was at work, and the victory was won.

A businessman in my church had been bidding on a very large contract. He had spent many hours preparing the bid, plus the time he travelled from his office to theirs. He was very patient and believed that he was going to get the contract; he was sure he would! The news came that the contract was given to another company. Needless to say he was disappointed about the whole thing. He did not despair, though. He remembered a message that I had taught, "Stand Up And Live," and began to encourage himself with the Word. Faith, confidence, and hope began to rise up within him.

He called the firm and told them that he would like for his company to do the installation on this project. They were surprised that he would call and even talk to them, much less ask to do the work. His attitude was positive, and they called him back to do the installation. This job turned out to be the biggest job that his company had ever done up to that point. As an added benefit, the negotiating experience and business contracts that he obtained in this just recently brought him a contract for over 2 million dollars. He could have become angry and given up, especially after all the hours he had put into the contract, but he instead decided to stand up and live. When he did, God gave him favor, and the job was won.

DON'T BE AFRAID

Another of Satan's weapons against the believer is fear. Actually he tries to intimidate you with his attacks. He would prefer for you to worry instead of rest.

"Come unto me, all ye that labour and are heavy laden, and I will give you rest." [Matthew 11:28]

When you are walking in the Word, Satan can threaten you, but you do not have to be intimidated by it. The word **intimidate** means to make timid, or to cow down, to force or deter with threats of violence. When you are walking or living by faith, and standing for different things, Satan will try to intimidate you. In other words, he will threaten you with circumstances, putting negative thoughts in your mind, to get you to be timid or to cow down to him.

127

If you let his threats get to you, then despondency will be next. You will lose your courage, hope, and confidence. This is the opposite of patience; and when you lose patience, Satan begins to move in. The result is that you do not get your answer, and you begin to feel sorry for yourself. You usually say, "I don't understand why this has happened to me. I've stood, I've prayed, I've confessed, but look at me—nobody cares, etc." You have let it happen by listening to Satan's lies. Don't let him threaten you. Put the Word to work on him and stand your ground!

"...but, he that is begotten of God keepeth himself, and that wicked one toucheth him not." [I John 5:18]

Keep yourself from the threats of Satan. You are begotten of God, and Satan can't touch you unless you let him. God has not given you a spirit of fear, but one of **love** and a **sound** mind; and perfect love will cast out any and all fear.

"Fear not; [there is nothing to fear] for I am with you; do not look around you in terror and be dismayed, for I am your God. I will strengthen and harden you [to difficulties]; yes, I will help you; yes, I will hold you up and retain you with My victorious right hand of rightness and justice." [Isaiah 41:10, Amplified]

As you continue to encourage yourself in the Lord, you are strengthened; and as you exercise your patience, you become immune to difficulties. As you walk by **FAITH** and not by sight, you do not look at the problem or the difficult situations but at the end result.

Even though you know what the situation is at the present time, you know the spirit of God is bringing change to the situation.

"...first the blade, then the ear, after that the full corn in the ear." [Mark 4:28]

It takes time for your faith to produce the end result. Don't let Satan cause you to fear and cow down. Give the answer time to come. Plant the seed, water it by meditating in and praying the Word, and it *will* grow to maturity...**BUT NOT OVERNIGHT!**

Don't be afraid. **God is faithful.** He has given you His faith, His power, His love, His wisdom, and His Spirit.

"For God has not given us the spirit of fear; but of power, and of love, and of a sound mind." [II Timothy 1:7]

Fear is not God. It is meditating and worrying about the things that you **don't** want to happen. God does not give you fear but love, confidence, and hope. So don't listen to Satan's threats.

"Finally, brethren, whatsoever things are true, whatsoever things are honest, whatsoever things are just, whatsoever things are pure, whatsoever things are lovely, whatsoever things are of good report; if there be any virtue, and if there be any praise, think on these things." [Philippians 4:8]

Satan will try to cause you to doubt God's ability to keep His Word, and this will hinder your faith and patience. Meditate on the answer and be persistent. GIVE GOD TIME TO WORK IN YOUR BEHALF.

There is a time and a season for everything. Many people want things to happen overnight and give up if they don't see a physical change overnight. Remember, a house is not built overnight, and a child is not developed overnight. I am not telling you to expect many months or years to pass before you see results. NO...EXPECT IT *NOW,* see it *NOW.* Stand and watch it develop. Some things take time for your faith to develop or mature.

I believe that many pastors have been discouraged, because they have seen the seeming "instant success" of other pastors. Their churches are small, and their growth is nothing compared to others. It is a mistake to look at another church, city, or state; and compare yours to theirs. If you are in that category, it may be wise to see what a "successful" pastor is doing. It could be that you are making some mistakes which are hindering your growth, but it could also be that the pastor of the church which has grown so rapidly is reaping seed that has been sown by others. The pastor of the church that is growing slowly may have to first plow up the fallow ground, tradition, religious spirits, etc., before he can begin to sow in good soil. It could be that no one has ever been in that area teaching the Uncompromised Word before.

In the previous example, faith and patience will surely pay off. If you are a pastor or member of a church that is not growing as fast as others, don't get discouraged if you are doing all you know to do. Your seeds *will come up!* Everything I say is a seed. Every radio spot, every newspaper ad, *everything is a seed!* It may not come up for years...**BUT** it will; I always reap.

Remember, don't be in a hurry.

I remember when I first moved back to Chattanooga, Tennessee. I decided that I wanted to begin an exercise program and joined a local health spa. I told the instructor that I wanted a larger chest, smaller waist, stronger legs, and bigger biceps; but I didn't want a big neck. He measured me, weighed me, and prescribed the proper regimen. He said, "I want you to start with this program, and as you get used to it, we will increase the weight, and number of repetitions." I agreed and went to the gym floor where he took me through each set of exercises. At the end, he said, "You're finished for the day, and you can go to the steam room, swimming pool, etc. I'll see you day after tomorrow."

When we finished, I didn't feel tired or out of breath. I began to look around and see those who had been on a program for several years. Everywhere I looked, I saw all of these people who had developed powerful muscles. As they walked around, I would look at them—and then at myself. I said to myself, "I need a better work out. I haven't done enough." I went back to the weights, added more, did more repititions, then flexed my muscles in the mirror. I did this repeatedly - over and over. I could just see myself getting larger, but as I continued, I became so weak my legs shook when I walked.

I went to the steam room and the whirlpool; and by the time I got out of the whirlpool, I could barely make it to the shower. After I dressed I struggled to the snack shop and asked for a drink that would give me some energy. Boy, was I weak and feeling bad! After a few minutes, I could finally get to the car. When I got home Sharon said, "What happened to you?" I said, "I got muscles." Well...I had to lie down to regain my strength. I also had to drink more and eat just to sit up. By bedtime, I was feeling a little better. I went over to the mirror, pulled my t-shirt off, and began to flex my muscles. I said to Sharon, "Look how big my chest biceps are!" She replied, "Oh, why don't you go to bed." She was not very impressed.

Needless to say, when I got up the next morning the only thing that would move were my eyelids. I was so sore, Sharon had to help me out of the bed. I hurt so badly. I sat in a hot tub for thirty minutes, before I could walk. What I was trying to do was get muscles overnight. I learned the hard way that it does not come that way—**IT TAKES TIME!** I was told what to do and knew better, but I ignored my instructor and suffered. He showed me the proper way to keep me from getting sore and wearing out, but I wanted muscles **now!** Even though I did extra work and went through *much pain,* it did not help; I only felt worse.

What I am telling you is to take God's Word and apply it every day. Give the word time to grow and let patience have her perfect work. The result is that you will be fully equipped, wanting nothing! Patience must be active in the life of the believer for him to be able to come into maturity. Have a plan. Continue to follow it, and you will get through by your faith and patience.

Chapter 10

THE IMPORTANCE OF PRAYER

Prayer should not be looked upon as an obligation or something that a Christian must do. Prayer is an opportunity; it is something you are privileged to do. It should not be put off, be dreaded, or become a bondage to anyone; because by praying, you are communicating and in fellowship with God. When I speak on the subject of prayer, I tell people that I look forward to prayer just as I look forward to spending time with my family. When we have an evening together, it is a great opportunity to be together and enjoy each other's company. I rise early most every morning, and pray out of a desire to spend time with the Father, not out of obligation. As I do so, my relationship with God is strengthened, my vision is renewed, and I am greatly encouraged.

To develop into a mature Christian one will recognize the importance of prayer and will not put it off. He will understand that it is a vital part of his life. One who dreads prayer or puts it off has never really learned how to communicate or fellowship with God. Prayer, to him, is labor. Prayer to the spiritually mature Christian is one of the most refreshing, rewarding times of his day.

There are those who tell me, "I pray all the time; when I'm riding in my car on the way to work, or to church..., etc." I agree that this is good and don't stop if you do, but set aside a time each day that is just between you and the Father. If you are married, you know that you do not talk to your spouse only when you're traveling in the car. **No!** A strong relationship between a husband and wife is built by the quality time that they spend sharing with each other.

Let me encourage you here that if you do not have a consistent prayer life to think about it. Plan on doing something about it; begin to pray daily. Just as you eat regularly to have strength to go through the day, your prayer life is *just as* important. I'm sure that you don't eat out of obligation. No; you enjoy eating. Prayer should be the same way in the life of every believer.

I'm not the kind of teacher who would tell you to do as I say and not as I do. No, I say "Do as I do." I am a praying person, and this is not a boastful statement. I pray, therefore I feel qualified to encourage you to do the same. I was born again when I was fifteen years old. My mother was a praying person. She loved to pray and still does. I learned to pray from my mother. Prayer works -- it pays off!

HOW DO I PRAY?

*"And in that day ye shall ask me nothing.
Verily, verily, I say unto you, Whatsoever ye
shall ask the Father in my name, he will give it
you." [John 16:23]*

Jesus was saying here that after the resurrection, you can't physically ask Him anything, but whatever you ask the Father in Jesus name, He (God) will give it to you.

Anything that you ask should be done in Jesus' name. The name of Jesus is like a key that unlocks a door. When you understand the power and authority in His name, you can see all of heaven standing to attention when you pray in the name of Jesus. E.W. Kenyon once said when you pray in the name of Jesus, it is the same as if He was here doing the praying Himself.

*"And whatsoever ye do in word or deed, do all
in the name of the Lord Jesus, giving thanks to
God and the Father by him." [Colossians 3:17]*

Each time you come to the Father for anything, it should be done in Jesus' name, not Jesus' sake. Using the name of Jesus in everything you do is like having power of attorney. In other words, as a Christian, the name of Jesus has been given to you to use daily in your prayers. Then when you pray in Jesus' name, your prayers are received by the Father, because the name of Jesus is your legal entry into the throneroom!

PRAY BY FAITH

I've heard some people say, "I pray; but when I do it feels like I am hitting a brick wall." Think for a moment on that statement. What difference does it make what it "feels" like? The Bible does not say that God hears you when you feel like He does. No! You come to Him, not by how you feel, but by what you believe. Whether you feel like it or not has no bearing on God's hearing you. When you come to the Father in the name of Jesus, He always hears you if you are praying in faith. Before Jesus raised Lazarus from the dead, He prayed this prayer:

"...*Father, I thank thee that thou hast heard me.*

42, And I know that thou hearest me always: but because of the people which stand by I said it, that they may believe that thou hast sent me." *[John 11:41 & 42]*

Just as Jesus said, "I know that thou hearest me always...", the spiritual adult should know that his prayers are always heard when he prays in faith according to the will of God.

"*And this is the confidence that we have in him, that, if we ask any thing according to his will, he heareth us:*

15, And if we know that he hears us, whatsoever we ask, we know that we have the petitions that we desired of him." *[I John 5:14 & 15]*

When you know what you are asking for is in agreement with God's word, you know that it is not a selfish petition. You can have the confidence that your prayers are heard and that you will receive what you ask for. It is that simple.

> *"Therefore I say unto you, What things soever ye desire, when we pray, believe that ye receive them, and ye shall have them." [Mark 11:24]*

Jesus said in this verse that you can have what you desire...**IF** you believe. Remember this. When you pray, you must ask in faith in order to get your desires.

PRAY FOR THOSE IN AUTHORITY

> *"I exhort therefore, that, first of all, supplications, prayers, intercessions, and giving of thanks, be made for all men;*
> *2, For Kings, and for all that are in authority; that we may lead a quiet and peaceable life in all godliness and honesty." [I Timothy 2:1 & 2]*

Paul was saying that he exhorts you to pray for your leaders, because they have great responsiblities. You should pray that they will demonstrate integrity, walk in wisdom, deal wisely in all issues, and help ensure that our freedom will be maintained in this country. You should pray that laborers will be sent to witness and minister to those in authority who are not born again. Also pray that wise counsel is given to them by men and women of God. Kings in the Old Testament called upon the Prophets, and many times God sent them with a message to the King. I believe that it should be the same now.

137

You should pray that the leaders who govern unjustly will be confused, and that God will raise up another one in their place. You should also pray that those who oppose God and His Son Jesus will fall from their position of power.

> *"Destroy thou them, O God; let them fall by their own counsels; cast them out in the multitude of their trangressions; for they have rebelled against thee." [Psalms 5:10]*

One of the ways in which revival will come to nations is by the government leaders having an experience with God. Paul said to pray for those in authority, and this includes those in the ministry. I believe you should pray for your Pastor every day, believing that he walks in the spirit of wisdom, the revelation knowledge of Jesus, and that his eyes will be enlightened by the Holy Spirit to always do the will of God.

The four other ministry gifts are as important to the body of Christ as the Pastor and should be included in your prayers also. Pray that there is perfect love between the five ministry gifts. Pray that there is no competition or strife, but all work in unity to accomplish the will of God in their lives and in the body of Christ.

Satan attacks the men and women of God who are in the ministry, and they need your prayers. You need to pray that they will not be caught off guard whenever the attacks come but will recognize what Satan is trying to do and not let him in. The five ministry gifts have been placed in the body to lead and minister depth; and as you pray for them, God will use them in a greater way to minister to your needs. Once again, you

138

will experience how God gives back to you.

PRAY FOR OTHERS

I want to point out here that it is really important for you to have compassion and concern for other people as you spend time praying for the needs. Also as you give to others by praying for them, healing will come to you, or the answer to your needs will manifest. It's a spiritual law. When you pray for people, God will cause others to begin to pray for you.

"Confess your faults one to another, and pray one for another, that ye may be healed. The effectual fervent prayer of a righteous man availeth much." [James 5:16]

Praying for others actually causes your faith to grow. As you release faith for the answer, you become excited about their needs being met. As a result you see the answers to your needs without much prayer.

Paul tells you in Ephesians 6:18 to pray for all saints. Many people will pray for their families, their circle of friends, and ministries that they know. However, God wants everyone to have a bigger vision and express love and compassion to more than a small circle. God wants you to pray for those in other denominations; people you don't know. Get involved and concerned in prayer about ministries which have not yet been spirit-filled or that you do not agree with. Pray for them, and God will minister to them. Everywhere I go, people come up to me and tell me that they pray for me all the time. It really blesses me. I know why my name is placed on their hearts. It is because so much of my prayer time is spent praying for others.

Many times as I have gone to prayer, I have been hurting and aching inside. However, instead of focusing on my needs, I gave attention to the needs of people in my church, others I've known in the ministry, friends, neighbors, and many whom I did not know very well. When I finished praying for them, the hurt would be gone. It was released as I prayed for others. Oh, what a joy to pray!

Spending quality time in prayer, fellowshipping with God, and praying for different people has been where I have matured a great deal. I have become closer to many people because of the time I spend in prayer for them. I have watched other people who have had a bad attitude towards me change as I spent time with God praying God's best for them.

If you have not developed a regular prayer time, I encourage you now to put aside some time each day for prayer. Don't wait until the end of the day or evening for your time with the Lord. You're too tired then and probably too sleepy. Pray when you are fresh and alert. Give your best to God. As you start your day with prayer, it will keep you in agreement with the Word of God *all day long.* If you will make a commitment to prayer, you will be more concerned about those around you through the day. One reason is because you have been praying for them in the morning, and each time you talk to them, it will remind you of your prayers. It will cause you to encourage them; and as you encourage them, it will edify you.

HAVE A PRAYER LIST

When you pray, make a list of the people you are going to pray for and the reason you are praying for them. Don't just ask God to bless so-and-so. Be specific. God has already blessed the believers with all spiritual blessings (Ephesians 1:3), but you must know how to bring these blessings into fruition. Also by having a prayer list, it will keep you from forgetting what you should pray for. Follow your list unless the Spirit leads you otherwise and don't look at the clock every few minutes to see how long you have prayed. Set aside a specific amount of time for prayer and give that time to God. When I pray at home I have a room where I go and do not take a clock. The time goes by quickly, because my mind is not on the time but on fellowshipping with God.

Make a commitment to pray which you can keep. If your commitment is 15 minutes, you can stay an extra 5 minutes, but your commitment has been for only 15 minutes. As this begins to work for you, raise your commitment 5 minutes, and stay an extra 5 minutes. I started with an hour, and stayed an extra 15 or 20 minutes, sometimes even an hour. I committed to what I knew I would keep, and prayer became a beautiful part of my life.

This chapter on prayer is not intended to teach on different kinds of prayer but to encourage you to incorporate prayer in your life so that you will develop into a mature Christian. I will discuss what I feel to be the most important areas of prayer.

When you go to prayer with your list, don't be

bound by it. Be sensitive to the Holy Spirit. He may have you pray differently. There may be someone in need who is not on your list. You may spend the entire time praying in tongues; but if you have a prayer list, it makes your prayers more structured when the Spirit does not lead you to pray in a different way.

When I begin praying, I pray for the leaders of the nation and other countries first. I follow by praying for those who are in the ministry; next, my church family; lastly, my family and myself. Most of the time I never get to me. This does not mean that I pray this way every day; however, if the Spirit does not change my direction, this is the general structure. I also spend much of my prayer time praying in tongues.

PRAY IN THE SPIRIT

"For if I pray in an [unknown] tongue, my spirit (by the Holy Spirit within me) prays, but my mind is unproductive—bears no fruit and helps nobody.

15, Then what am I to do? I will pray with my spirit—by the Holy Spirit that is within me; but I will also pray intelligently—with my mind and understanding; I will sing with my spirit—by the Holy Spirit that is within me; but I will sing (intelligently) with my mind and understanding also." [I Corinthians 14:14, Amplified]

Praying in the Spirit is praying in tongues. When you pray in tongues, it should be done in private, because you are speaking directly to God. Only God

142

understands what you are saying. He gives you a language to communicate with Him from your spirit, and it bypasses your intellect. You can pray in tongues that which you cannot put in words to tell the Father.

You do not understand what you are saying, but God does. He knows the thoughts and intents of your heart. So as you pray in tongues, it is the Spirit in control of your prayer. One of the great advantages of praying in the Holy Ghost is that Satan cannot understand what you are saying to God and, therefore, cannot hinder it.

"For he that speaketh in an unknown tongue speaketh not unto men, but unto God: for no man understandeth him; howbeit in the spirit he speaketh mysteries." [I Corinthians 14:2]

Here again Paul says that you are talking directly to God, and that mysteries are revealed. I would urge every person to spend time in prayer, especially pray in tongues. By doing so, revelation and direction will come for your **future**, your **marriage**, your **children**, your **ministry**, your **business**, or your **job**. God will show you exactly what you need to do.

Every man and woman should spend time with God praying in the Spirit so they will always know what God has in store for them. He will show you exactly what to do *if* you will give Him the opportunity. One of the great things about prayer is that you are not only talking to God, He is talking to you!

When you go to God in your native language or pray in the Holy Ghost, it builds you up. Prayer is like focusing the lens of a camera on the object you want to photograph. You want the object to be clear, not fuzzy

143

or distorted. As you turn the lens to the right setting, the object becomes focused, and you press the button on the camera to take the picture. As you pray in the Spirit, the direction for your day, week, month, and life becomes clearer. You become stronger to be able to go in the direction that God has for you. You get so built up in your faith that you can stand against the attacks of the enemy and be an overcomer in everything.

"But ye, beloved, building up yourselves on your most holy faith, praying in the Holy Ghost." [Jude 20]

The Spirit helps your weaknesses and makes intercession for you. I know that there are times when you don't know how to pray concerning a situation. The Holy Spirit knows just what to say. As you pray in tongues, the Spirit prays or says things which you can't put into your own words. There are also times when you are praying for others and really don't know how to pray for them. Praying in tongues eliminates your lack of knowledge, and the Spirit does what you wanted to do but couldn't.

"Likewise the Spirit also helpeth our infirmities: for we know not what we should pray for as we ought: but the Spirit itself maketh intercession for us with groanings which cannot be uttered." [Romans 8:26]

You are further admonished by Paul in I Thessalonians 5:17 to pray without ceasing. This is done by beginning your day with individual prayer and intercession, praying in tongues at every opportunity, rejoicing in spiritual songs and hymns, praying a prayer of agreement with someone, attending intercession at

144

your church, entering into a united prayer, or maybe choosing to spend the day in prayer and fasting. The believer looks for every opportunity to pray. Nothing on the flaky side but, instead, real communication with God.

> *"Pray at all times—on every occasion, in every season—in the Spirit, with all (manner of) prayer and entreaty. To that end keep alert and watch with strong purpose and perseverance, interceding in behalf of all the saints (God's consecrated people)." [Ephesians 6:18, Amplified]*

Paul exhorts you to pray at all times and with all manner of prayers. He is actually saying for you to pray the type of prayer that is needed for a specific need or time; whether it be a prayer of request [Mark 11:24], a united prayer [Acts 4:31-33], a prayer of worship and praise [Acts 13:2], the prayer of intercession [Romans 8:26], or a special time set aside for fasting and prayer [Matthew 17:20-21]. Paul is also saying not to just pray for yourself, but pray for whoever has a need. Be sensitive to the needs of others so that you can pray with all perseverance until you see the need met.

FASTING

Fasting should become a part of your life, not out of obligation but out of a desire to hear God's voice. Let me say here that fasting will not grant you the answer to your prayer, make God move for you, or give you more power. Fasting and prayer together helps make your mind and body quiet so you can hear the voice of the Spirit more easily. Faith will bring the answer, and you always have power. You just have to learn how to use that power.

Fasting does not bring you closer to God. When you are born again, you are as close as you can ever get. It is as your mind is renewed and you fully understand your righteousness that you become more conscious of the God who lives within you.

Fasting should be done in private. It should not be something that you tell people you are doing.

"But thou, when thou fasteth, anoint thine head, and wash thy face;

18, That thou appear not unto men to fast, but unto thy Father which is in secret: and thy Father, which seeth in secret, shall reward thee openly." [Matthew 6:17 & 18]

When you fast, you are not to have a sad countenance, so that others would look upon you. No, this is between you and the Lord.

To fast one, three, five, or even seven days, you do not need a special leading from God if you are physically strong enough. However, there should be a purpose in the fast, something that you want to hear or understand. Don't fast just to fast. If you are going to go on an extended fast, I believe that you should have a direct leading from God to do so. When Jesus fasted 40 days, He was led by the Spirit.

"Then was Jesus led up of the spirit into the wilderness to be tempted of the devil.

2, And when he had fasted forty days and forty nights, he was afterward an hungered." [Mat-

thew 4:1 & 2]

Jesus was led by the Spirit to do so, and so should you.

When I operated in the ministry gift of an evangelist, I spent a lot of time in prayer and fasting. I have fasted as much as forty days, but it was through the direction of the Holy Spirit. On many occasions I have been led to fast 21 days, 14 days, 10 days, and so on, but **God** led me to do so, and I always had results from it. During those times my mind and body became so tuned into God, great revivals and miracles took place.

In closing this chapter, I trust that I've said something here that will inspire you to pray more. I love to pray and cherish each moment that I have alone in my prayer closet. I enjoy the times of prayer with other people and riding in my car praying in tongues. The time that I shut the door in the morning and am alone with God, though, is what I look forward to most in life. Remember what Jesus said:

"...The effectual fervant prayer of a righteous man availeth much." [James 5:16]

147

148

Chapter 11

FELLOWSHIP

Fellowship is very important in the life of every believer. Your spiritual growth depends a lot upon your fellowship with God and other believers in the body of Christ. Believers need to attend church regularly to get a steady diet of the Word of God. Some think that it is just as good to get teaching from tapes or staying home and watching television. **THERE IS A BIG DIF-FERENCE!** You need to be where the meeting is going on. Staying at home and having bedside assembly does not equate with being at church.

Not only do you need to go to church to hear the Word; but you also need fellowship with other believers. People need people of "like" faith. I've had people tell me, "Our family fellowships together." This is good and you should. I'm glad that your family is close enough that they fellowship together, but **there**

are other believers who need you too. There are many in the body of Christ whom you could share with, bring encouragement to, and help by fellowshipping with them. You need other believers, and as this chapter progresses, I will show you through the word just how much.

CALLED IN FELLOWSHIP

"God is faithful, by whom ye were called unto the fellowship of his Son Jesus Christ our Lord." [I Corinthians 1:9]

You fellowship with God through prayer, meditating in the Word, and singing songs in the Spirit. You also fellowship with Him when you spend time with other believers. When you fellowship with one another, you strengthen one another. The scripture says that you are called unto the fellowship of his Son Jesus Christ our Lord. There are many members of the body of Christ, and everyone has kinship and a responsibility to each other. When you are born again, you become a part of the family of God. Actually, every person in the body is related to each other through Jesus Christ, so you should desire fellowship with other believers outside of your immediate family. Why? Because your family now includes people of all races and nationalities. It's the one that God sees.

"For as the body is one, and hath many members, and all the members of that one body, being many, are one body: so also is Christ.

13, For by one Spirit are we all baptized into

one body, whether we be Jews or Gentiles,
whether we be bond or free; and have been all
made to drink into one Spirit.

14, For the body is not one member, but many.

15, If the foot shall say, Because I am not the
hand, I am not of the body; is it therefore not of
the body?

16, And if the ear shall say, Because I am not
the eye, I am not of the body; is it therefore not
of the body?

17, If the whole body were an eye, where were
the hearing? If the whole were hearing, where
were the smelling?

18, But now hath God set the members every
one of them in the body, as it hath pleased him.

19, And if they were all one member, where
were the body?

20, But now are they many members, yet but
one body.

21, And the eye cannot say unto the hand, I
have no need of thee: nor again the head to the
feet, I have no need of you.

22, Nay, much more those members of the
body, which seem to be more feeble, are
necessary:

23, And those members of the body, which we
think to be less honourable, upon these we
bestow more abundant honour; and our un-
comely parts have more abundant comeliness.

24, For our comely parts have no need: but God

> *hath tempered the body together, having given more abundant honour to that part which lacked:*
>
> *25, That there should be no schism in the body; but that the members should have the same care one for another.*
>
> *26, And whether one member suffer, all the members suffer with it; or one member be honoured, all the members rejoice with it."* [I Corinthians 12:12-26]

In verse 25, it says that the members of the body should have the same care for one another. Verse 26 says that if one member suffers, all the members suffer with it. Paul is saying that you should get to know other people in your local church and care for them. If they suffer, you should have compassion for them and help them. You are not to say, "Oh well, I don't know them." Make it your business to know them; and in this way, you will become aware of their needs.

In these verses of scripture Paul said that there are many members, but all make up the body. Every person has a place in the body and is needed. God has set everyone in the body as it has pleased Him, so find your place, fit in, and spend time fellowshipping with other believers. Don't say, "I have no need of you.' Just as you need every part of your physical body, you need all the different parts of the body of Christ.

Are you involved in a local church? If not, you should be. How many people in your church do you know? I'm talking about knowing them more than just seeing them at church, smiling at them, and shaking their hands. Do you know several people there wel

enough to minister to them if they are hurting? If you
don't, you should, and it's your responsibility. Do you
know five families intimately at your church? If not,
why? Some people say, "Well, I'm a private person,
and I don't want to get involved." The only way that
you can help other people and help yourself is by getting involved.

> *"...for what fellowship hath righteousness
> with unrighteousness? and what communion
> hath light with darkness?"* [II Corinthians
> 6:14]

Believers need to fellowship with other believers, not
with people of the world. When you fellowship with
other believers, your conversation will be edifying,
uplifting, and encouraging. I've seen a lot of divorces in
the church that would not have happened if the couple
would have had Godly friends. I have known many people who would not have become discouraged, quit
church, and grown cold if they would have had regular
fellowship with Godly friends. Because they did not
get involved, though, or no one offered to get them involved, they had no friends in the church to stand with
them when Satan attacked. I'm not suggesting for you
to have just five friends and form a clique. No, broaden
your scope and get to know and understand other
believers.

Some people say that it's the Pastor's job to visit
everyone. The Pastor can teach and minister God's
Word and love, but the body is to edify one another.
This has been a lot of the problem with church growth
and spiritual maturity. People depend too much on the
Pastor. He should feed the sheep with good food and

153

lead them, but people should be reproducing themselves by making other disciples. **Shepherds do not bear sheep—SHEEP BEAR SHEEP!**

Some are always late getting to church and miss some or all of the worship and praise. Many times it is intentional, because they don't want to talk to anyone. These same people will also leave at the dismissal prayer; they don't want to get caught. They feel they may have to get involved. When there is a social function, they will not show up. Once again, they push away their responsibility.

Love will get involved. Love will commit to help others because love is not selfish. A person who does not want to get involved or fellowship with others is selfish and will never mature to the better things of God. When people spend time together encouraging and sharing with one another, the vision of the Pastor is strengthened. If there is a weakness in one believer, another will be stronger and able to lift up the other one. People will begin to develop in other areas, because they see the Christian life truly working.

THE EARLY CHURCH FELLOWSHIPPED

"And they continued steadfastly in the apostles' doctrine and fellowship, and in breaking of bread, and in prayers." [Acts 2:42]

Paul said that the people were committed and loyal to the Apostles' doctrine, they fellowshipped one with another, and they spent time eating together.

"I thank my God, making mention of thee always in my prayers,

154

5, Hearing of thy love and faith, which thou hast toward the Lord Jesus, and toward all saints;

6, That the communication of thy faith may become effectual by the acknowledging of every good thing which is in you in Christ.

7, For we have great joy and consolation in thy love, because the bowels of the saints are refreshed by thee, brother." [Philemon 4-7]

In Paul's letter to Philemon, he was telling him how he had heard many good reports of how he (Philemon) had communicated his faith, and how others had been refreshed by his love. Paul, too, had been refreshed by his love. He exhorted Philemon to be kind to Onesimus, to show him love, and spend time fellowshipping with him, because Onesimus had the need for fellowship. Paul told him not to do it because he asked him to or out of bondage, but to do it out of love. He said, in other words, "Philemon, take the time to disciple Onesimus."

As Philemon was exhorted by Paul to disciple Onesimus, I exhort you to fellowship and disciple with other people. Don't let it be a bondage, but instead a joy. You can read the entire chapter of Philemon and see how Philemon had love towards the saints. As he acknowledged the good things that were in him, he refreshed the saints. Likewise, as you acknowledge the good things in you and others around you, you will build up yourself and those around you.

As you begin to spend time together with other believers, you will broaden your circle of friends and help people outside your existing circle. You will find yourself looking for someone to minister to.

> *"For I am planning to take a trip to Spain, and when I do, I will stop off there in Rome; and after we have a good time together for a little while, you can send me on my way again.*
>
> *25, But before I come, I must go down to Jerusalem to take a gift to the Jewish Christians there.*
>
> *26, For you see, the Christians in Macedonia and Achaia have taken up an offering for those in Jerusalem who are going through such hard times. [Romans 15:24-26, The Living Bible]*

You can see in the verses above that, as people fellowship together, they not only meet the needs of the ministry, but they also help others in the body of Christ who have needs. The one who needs help could be you and because you are fellowshipping regularly, others will be sensitive to your needs and help you. It may be financial; it may be physical. God will bless people who are involved.

> *"A man that hath friends must shew himself friendly; and there is a friend that sticketh closer than a brother." [Proverbs 18:24]*

People who do not go out of their way to show love and be friendly will have few friends. Godly friends are treasures. Some people say, "I don't have any friend at church. No one likes me." Do you show yourself friendly? When you are friendly with people, they will be friendly with you. **Everyone needs Godly friends!**

In 1982, my son Jeff was electrocuted and went home to be with Jesus. His departure from this life left

Sharon and me with pain and emptiness. Our friends came to us, cleaned our house, washed clothes, and cooked for us for several weeks. God was our source, but our friends allowed us to lean on them. They understood us as we hurt. Thank God for the Godly friends who helped us when we needed it; they were closer than a brother.

"*...and there is a friend that sticketh closer than a brother.*" *[Proverbs 18:24]*

Invest in other people; it will always come back to you.

FELLOWSHIP REGULARLY

"*Let us hold fast the profession of our faith without wavering; (for he is faithful that promised;)*

24, And let us consider one another to provoke unto love and to good works:

25, Not forsaking the assembling of ourselves together, as the manner of some is; but exhorting one another: and so much the more, as ye see the day approaching." *[Hebrews 10:23-25]*

Don't let Satan or circumstances keep you from attending church regularly. The Word says not to forsake the assembling yourselves together as some have. He said that when everyone comes together, it is a time to exhort each other and provoke one another to love and do good works.

Fellowship can be at church or many other places, but church should be your first priority. Just because you attend a Bible Study or go to a Teaching Center, it cannot take the place of having a Pastor. Everybody

157

needs a Pastor plus fellowship with the saints.

The word **fellowship** comes from the Greek word [koinonia] which means associate, participate, communicate, and intercourse. The word intercourse means to have communications or dealings between or among people; an interchange of products, services, or ideas. When believers are together in fellowship, there is a great opportunity to exchange ideas or communicate about things which you can help each other with.

When you fellowship with other members in the body of Christ, there is at least six things you do.

1. Associate — This word means to join together, unite, to join with others in some venture. When you begin to associate with a church, you agree with its doctrine and begin to make friends there.

2. Communication — This word means to impart, to share, to pass along, to make known, to give information. When believers associate and communicate, they impart life to each other by sharing and passing along their experiences. They share with each other how they have overcome in difficult times and give information that is helpful. When believers communicate, the Kingdom of God is built up, and the body of Christ becomes bigger and stronger. In Matthew 5, Jesus communicated to the disciples His doctrine. He gave them information which showed them how to live. Couples need other strong Christians to associate and communicate with. Widows, single, and divorced people need those in the Christian faith whom they can relate to. If you are in any of these categories, get in-

volved by fellowshipping with others; and by doing so, your needs, as well as the needs of others, will be met.

3. Participate — This word means to share with others in some activity. Christians should plan activities together such as witnessing, hospital visitation, helping someone with housework that has not been able to do it, helping the elderly, or possibly visiting a Nursing Home or prison. Plan to help each other fix a car together, help with plumbing or painting a house, join a Church ball team, go to a Couple's retreat, a church social, or a monthly get-together outside the church to participate with other belivers. As you participate with other strong believers, you become stronger.

"Two are better than one, because they have a good (more satisfying) reward for their labor;

10, For if they fall, the one will lift up his fellow. But woe to him who is alone when he falls and has not another to lift him up!

11, Again, if two lie together, then they have warmth; but how can one be warm alone?

12, And though a man might prevail against him who is alone, two will withstand him. A threefold cord is not quickly broken." [Ecclesiastes 4:9-12, Amplified]

4. Cooperate — This word means a joint effort or interaction. When you fellowship with others outside your immediate family, you begin to cooperate in a joint effort to take a city. You also help support the Pastor by two, three, or more getting together and

planning how to bless and encourage the Pastor and others in the church. As you bless them, others will bless you. You are in agreement with the vision, and join with others to accomplish the goals of the church. This also allows others to stand in agreement with you.

"Again I say unto you, That if two of you shall agree on earth as touching anything that they shall ask, it shall be done for them of my Father which is in heaven.

20, For where two or three are gathered in my name, there am I in the midst of them." [Matthew 18:19 & 20]

When you are in agreement with the Word, and others are in agreement with you, anything you ask will be done. Think about this. As you fellowship, not only by coming to church, but also by spending quality time with other believers, you can **together** accomplish great things.

5. Edify — This word means to instruct, improve, or build. When believers spend time doing things together, going places together, eating with each other, and helping each other, they are built up in spiritual areas. As the outside world looks at this, you are seen as a light and witness to them. Remember, if you are weak, associate with someone who is stronger than you. Don't make your circle so small that you only have two or three friends. Broaden your circle and have many friends. Don't follow people; follow Jesus. Let others inspire and edify you, but make your own decisions and be led by the Spirit.

"Let us therefore follow after the things which

> *make for peace, and things wherewith one may*
> *edify another. [Romans 14:19]*

When you build up others, you build up yourself. It is always rewarding to edify and strengthen others, see them advance in the kingdom of God, and see them mature to the place where they can trust God for themselves.

6. Celebrate — This word means to make a happy occasion by engaging in pleasurable activity. The world is always celebrating something. I believe that this is one of the places where Christians have missed out. They many times close themselves up with their immediate family and don't go out or do anything to get involved in the lives of others. They in turn lose their joy. Find something to celebrate, invite several couples over to your home, and make it an exciting evening. There are those who think that a Christian is supposed to do nothing but pray. I believe that there is a time to pray and there is a time when believers should come together to have fun. This could be the celebraton of a natural birthday or a spiritual birthday. There are plenty of things which Christians can celebrate if they will take the time to do so. Call someone up, go out, and celebrate like Christians do (without wine and strong drink).

In this book, I have not intended for the different chapters to be steps into spiritual maturity but more of incorporating all of them into your daily life. Some of these things you may already be doing; however, you may lack in other areas. As you read and study this book, I exhort you to find the place(s) where you may fall short and fill it (them).

This book has not just been taken from messages that I have preached and later transcribed. I have taken the time to sit down and put myself into these pages — share parts of my life, both mistakes and victories that I have had. I trust that by showing you where I have been to where I am now was and is a maturing process. My life is now what it is, because I have learned to be patient. This growth does not come overnight; it is a continual development process. One thing is for sure...I will continue growing! I believe that as you apply the simple truths that lie in the pages of this book, you, too, will continue to grow and mature to be like Jesus.

TAPE OF TODAY CLUB

Now you can have weekly messages as they are taught by Don Clowers sent to your home. A number of options are available to you under this tape subscription plan.

[ ] AM Messages only - $12.00 per month
[ ] PM Messages only - $12.00 per month
[ ] Both AM and PM - $20.00 per month

Check the option which you prefer above and your subscription will begin upon receipt of your order and two (2) months advance payment to establish the account. As account funds are drawn upon, a renewal invoice will be sent each month to replenish the account prior to fund depletion. NO RENEWAL ASSUMES CANCELLATION. Tapes will begin the week following receipt of order. Please enclose full payment. Check or money order only. Do not send cash.

NAME_____

ADDRESS_____

CITY_____ STATE_____ ZIP_____

Please print your name and address and make checks payable to:

Don Clowers Ministries, Inc.
P.O. Box 21389
Chattanooga, Tennessee 37421

BOOK AND TAPE LIST BY DON CLOWERS

SINGLES: $4.00

21017A . . . . Stand Up And Live
31002A . . . . Wait, Renew, Mount-Up, Walk, Run
31211A . . . . If It's Going To Be It's Up To Me
40226A . . . . Overcoming Failure
40325A . . . . The Importance of Regular Fellowship
40408A . . . . Push Forward, Break Out, Go Over

TWO TAPE ALBUMS: $8.00

30724A . . . . Position, Power, Purpose
31106A . . . . I Want My House Back
10308A . . . . How to End Your Money Problems
11213S . . . . The Anointing
20512A . . . . Weeds or Flowers

THREE TAPE ALBUMS: $12.00

10222A . . . . Limited or Unlimited
31130P . . . . Intercessory Prayer
30602P . . . . The Diligent Shall Rule

FIVE TAPE ALBUM: $20.00

11011A . . . . God is no Child Abuser

SIX TAPE ALBUM: $24.00

30105P . . . . The Christian Family

Item	Price	Quantity	Total
		Total	

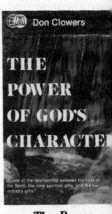

The Power of God's Character
By: Don Clowers

Price $5.50 each

Terms: Check or Money Order only. Do not send cash. Full payment must accompany all orders. Please allow minimum of 30 days for delivery.

164

King – get your house back